PROSPERITY

How to Attract It

BY

ORISON SWETT MARDEN

Author of "How to Get What You Want," "Heading
for Victory," "Peace, Power, and Plenty," etc.

SUCCESS MAGAZINE CORPORATION

PUBLISHERS

1133 BROADWAY,   NEW YORK, N. Y.

To OUR VERY DEAR FRIEND
MRS. ELISE DE VERE GODSOL

CONTENTS

PROSPERITY
HOW TO ATTRACT IT

CHAPTER I

HOW WE LIMIT OUR SUPPLY

"A man will remain a ragpicker as long as he has only a rag-picker's vision."

Why go thru life exhibiting the traits of an underling? If you are a real man, don't go around looking like a beggar, talking like a beggar, acting like a beggar.

Only by thinking prosperity and abundance can you realize the abundant, prosperous life.

Fixing limitation upon ourselves is one of the cardinal sins of mankind.

Prosperity flows only through channels that are wide open to receive it. Doubt, fear and lack of confidence close these channels.

A pinched mind means a pinched, limited supply.

Everything we get in life comes through the gateway of our thought. If that is pinched, stingy, mean, what flows to us will correspond.

WHAT would you think of a prince, the heir to a kingdom of limitless wealth and power, who should live in the condition of a pauper, who should go about the world bemoaning his hard fate and telling people how poor he was, saying that he didn't believe his father was going to leave him anything, and that he might as well make up his mind to a life of poverty and limitations?

You would say, of course, that he must be insane, and that his hard conditions, his poverty and limitations, were not actual, but imaginary; that they existed only in his mind; that his father was ready to load him with good things, with all that his heart desired, if he would only open his mind to the truth and live in the condition befitting a prince, the son and heir of a great king.

Now, if you are living in pinching poverty, in a narrow, cramped, limited environment in which there seems to be no hope, no outlook for better things; if you are not getting what you want, though working hard for it, you are just as foolish as the prince who, believing that he was poor, lived like a pauper in the midst of his father's limitless wealth. Your limitations are in your mind, just as the prince's were in his. You are the child of a Father who has created abundance, limitless wealth, for all of His children, but your pinched, limited, poverty-stricken thought shuts you out from all this abundance and keeps you in poverty.

A Russian laborer named Mihok, living in Omaha, Nebraska, had carried a "luck" stone in his pocket for twenty years, never guessing that it had any monetary value. Time and again friends, who thought that it might be more than an ordinary stone, suggested that he have it examined by a jeweler. He obstinately refused until, finally, they became so insistent that he sent the stone to a Chicago jeweler, who pronounced it a pigeon-blood ruby, the largest of its kind in the world. It weighed 24 karats and was worth $100,000!

There are millions like this poor day laborer, living in poverty, thinking that there is nothing for them but hard work and more poverty who, without knowing it, are carrying in the great within of themselves possibilities of wealth beyond their dreams. Their wrong thinking is robbing them of their divine inheritance; shutting off the abundant supply provided for them by the Omnipotent Source of all supply.

The majority of people are in the position of a man who went out to water his garden, but inadvertently stepped on the hose, shutting off the water supply. He had a big hose and was very much annoyed, very much disappointed, because he was getting only a mere dribble of water when he had every right to expect—and should get—a liberal flow. Water was at the source in abundance, ready to supply his needs; only one thing was at fault, the man himself was pinching his supply, limiting it to a miserable drizzle. He was standing on the hose and didn't know it.

That is literally what all who are living in grinding poverty are doing. They are pinching their supply by stepping upon the hose through which plenty would come to them. They are stopping the flow of abundance that is their birthright, by their doubts, their fears, their unbelief; by visualizing poverty, thinking poverty, acting as if they never expected to have anything, to accomplish anything, or to be anything.

Everything in man's life, everything in God's universe, is based upon principle—follows a divine law; and the law of prosperity and abundance is just as definite as the law of gravitation, just as unerring as the principles of mathematics. It is a mental law. Only by thinking abundance can you realize the abundant, prosperous life that is your birthright; in other words, according to your thought will be your life, your supply, or your lack. Your mental attitude will be flung back to you, every time, in kind. A poverty-stricken mental attitude will bring only poverty-stricken conditions to you.

We are the creatures of our convictions. We cannot get beyond what we believe we are; what we believe we have. Hence, if we think that we are never going to be strong or well like other people, or to be successful in our calling, we never will be. If we are convinced that we will always be poor, we will be. You can't get away from poverty when you don't expect to; when you don't believe that you are going to.

Many of the people who are living in poverty to-day never really expect anything else. Their fixed belief that they can never become prosperous keeps them in poverty; that is, it keeps their minds negative, and the mind cannot create, cannot produce, in this condition. It is only the positive mind that can create prosperity; the negative mind is noncreative, non-productive; it can only tear down, inhibit, prevent the inflow of the good things that we long for.

It is not so much what you do with your hands as what you do with your mind that counts. Everything that has been accomplished by the hand or brain of man had its birth in the mind. The universe itself is the creation of Divine Mind. A hard-working man who longs for prosperity, but is headed in the other direction mentally, who doesn't believe he is going to be prosperous, is neutralizing his hard work by his negative, destructive thought; he is standing on the hose that connects with his supply.

When you limit yourself in your thought, you are limiting yourself outwardly in a way which corresponds with your mental attitude, because you are obeying a law which is unchangeable. You will notice that the man who puts a nickel in the contribution box, is not only stingy, close, and mean in all his money matters, but his face, his whole person, has a cramped, worried, pinched look. He is forever saving pennies, watching out for little things and never doing big things. No matter how much natural ability he has, his narrow, limited, poverty thought dwarfs him and cuts off his stream of supply. He cannot do big things because he never thinks big things. His warped mind will admit only a pinched supply instead of the big flow that is literally at his command.

It is because we have not learned how to use our thought forces that most of us go about like paupers, never glimpsing the marvelous inheritance left us by the All-supply, the All-good. Our parsimonious thought pinches our supply.

We often wonder why it is that certain people, in apparently no better circumstances than we are, get so much better things than we do; why they always insist upon and receive the best of everything. We never see them wearing cheap things—never see cheap things in their homes, or any pinching anywhere. They buy the best food, the best fruits and vegetables in the market, and everything else in accordance. We think they are extravagant when we compare what they pay for things with what we pay for things of the same kind, and we pride ourselves that we are economizing and saving what they are wasting. But, are we? How does our manner of living compare with theirs? Does the enjoyment we get out of life measure up to what they get? Do the few dollars we save compensate for the great lack in our lives—the lack of good food, of proper clothing, of the little pleasure trips, the social enjoyments, the picnics and various diversions which make life pleasant, healthful, and above all, much more productive for the neighbors whose extravagance we condemn? As a matter of fact, our skimped, pinching policy leaves us poorer in the end.

Prosperity flows only through channels that are wide open to receive it. It does not flow through channels pinched by the poverty thought, by discouragement, doubt, or fear, or by a strangling narrow-visioned policy. A generous expenditure is often the wisest economy, the only thing that brings a generous success. If a great manufacturer like Henry Ford, a great merchant like John Wanamaker, a big railroad manager, or other business man, should lose his broad vision and wide outlook; should begin to skimp on necessary output; should substitute inferior goods and men and service for the best; should reverse his policy, changing from a broad, generous one to a narrow, stingy one, he would soon find his business dwindling away to nothing.

There is no changing the principle of the law of supply. Whatever your business, your profession or occupation, or your circumstances, your mental attitude will determine your success or failure. A pinched mind means a pinched supply. It means that you try to tap the great fountainhead of supply with a gimlet and then expect to get an abundant supply. That is impossible. Your mental attitude gauges the flow of your supply.

CHAPTER II

THE LAW OF ATTRACTION

By the law of affinity you may know that your own is always seeking you if you are seeking it with all your might and are not driving it away with your doubts.

John Burroughs thus beautifully expressed this:

"I rave no more 'gainst Time or Fate,
For lo, my own shall come to me.
* * *
"Asleep, awake, by night or day,
The friends I seek are seeking me.

"What matter if I stand alone?
I wait with joy the coming years;
My heart shall reap where it hath sown,
What is mine shall know my face.
* * *
"Nor time, nor space, nor deep, nor high
Can keep my own away from me."

IT was never intended that God's children should ever want for anything. We live in the very lap of abundance; there is plenty of everything all about us, the great cosmic universe is packed with all sorts of beautiful, marvelous things, glorious riches, ready for our use and enjoyment. Everything the hu-

10

man heart can crave, the great creative Intelligence offers us. We can draw from this vast ocean of intelligence everything we wish: all that it is necessary for us to do is to obey the law of attrac ion,—like attracts like.

To realize prosperity and abundance does not depend upon man's own little brain, his own little one-sided efforts. It is a question of his making his mind a magnet to attract the things he wants, to attract his desires.

Everything that the race enjoys has been attracted out of the great ocean of intelligence according to a law. All inventions, all discoveries, all the marvelous facilities of civilization,—our hospitals, our schools, our churches, our libraries, and other institutions, our homes, with their comforts and luxuri .,—have all been attracted from this great cosmic storehouse of intelligence by the same law.

It was intended that our longings, our yearnings, our legitimate desires should be satisfied, that our dreams should come true. It is our ignorance of the law that would bring our own to us which keeps it from us.

When you were a boy experimenting with your little steel magnet, didn't you often try to make it pick up wood, copper, rubber, or some other substance different from itself? And, of course, you found it would not, because it had no affinity for things that were unlike itself. You found that it would pick up a needle but not a toothpick. In other words you demonstrated the law that—*Like attracts like.*

Not a day passes that we do not see this law demonstrated in different ways in human life. Sometimes the demonstrations are very tragic. Only a short time ago a little eight-year-old girl, the daughter of a Pennsylvania farmer, died from fright in a dentist's chair, where she had been placed to have a tooth extracted. Although the child knew nothing about the law, it worked just the same; and, like Job, the thing she feared had come to her.

By the operation of the same law that draws to us disease and death, we draw to ourselves poverty or opulence, success or failure. The mind at any given time is a magnet for something. It is a magnet for whatever thought, whatever convictions dominate the mind at the time, and the blessed, glorious thing about it all is that we can determine what the mind shall attract, what sort of a magnet it shall become. Now, you may attract to you that which is not good for you, that which will damn you, that which will pain and humiliate. By concentrating upon and working for it you become a specialist in that line and the law of attraction brings it to you.

If you have a prosperity mental attitude, if you have a vigorous faith that you are going to get away from poverty, that you are going to demonstrate prosperity, abundance, and strive intelligently and persistently to realize your vision, you will do so. That's the law. If you obey the law you will get good results.

If we could only see a picture of the mental processes of whatever is held in the mind, pulling the things which correspond to our thought; if we could see more failure, more bad business, more debts, more losses starting towards us because we have contacted with these things in our thought, we would quit worrying about the things we don't want and think the things we do want, attracting more instead of less, attracting abundance instead of poverty, prosperity instead of failure.

Oh, how often we make our mind a magnet to attract all sorts of enemy thoughts, poverty thoughts, sick thoughts, fear thoughts, and worry thoughts, and then somehow we expect that a miracle will be performed, and that out of these negative causes we will be sure in some way to enjoy positive results. No miracle could perform such a change as this. Results correspond with causes.

Before we can be conquered by poverty, we must, first of all, be poor mentally. The poverty thought, the acceptance of a poverty-stricken environment as an inevitable condition from which you cannot get away, keeps you in the poverty current and draws more poverty to you. It is the operation of the same law which attracts good things, a better environment, to those who think abundance, prosperity, who are convinced that they are going to be well off, and work confidently, hopefully, toward that end.

Not the things we long for most, not the things we wish for, but our own, that which has lived in our thoughts and mind, dominated in our mentality, in our mental attitude, that is what the law of attraction brings to us. It may be that this law has brought us the very things we hated and wanted to get rid of, but we have dwelt upon them, and, because they formed the mental model, the life processes built them into our lives.

The law of attraction often brings us hated bedfellows, but they have lived so long in our minds, that they must become a part of our lives, by the very law that like attracts like.

Until recently many of us did not understand what Job meant when he said, "The thing which I greatly feared has come upon me." Now we know that he expressed a psychological law that is as inexorable as the laws of mathematics. We know that the things we fear most, the things we have a horror of and want to flee from, we are really pursuing by our very fear of them. By predicting them and visualizing them in our minds, we are attracting them to ourselves, and when we do this we are turning our backs upon the very things which we long for most.

The time will come when the law of attraction will be known as the greatest power in creation. This is the law upon which all successes, all characters, all lives are built. Mental attraction is the only power upon which we can build anything successfully. It is an inevitable law, an inexorable principle, that everything attracts to itself everything else like itself, that all affinities tend to get together, and when you make your mind a magnet it will attract according to its quality, according to your mental vision, your thoughts, your motives, your dominant attitude.

The saying "Money attracts money" is only another way of stating the law,—"like attracts like." The prosperous classes think prosperity, believe in it, work for it, never for a moment doubt their right to have all the money and all the good things they need, and of course they get them. They are living up to the very letter and spirit of the law of attraction. A Rockefeller, a Schwab, uses this law in a masterly way to amass a large fortune. The newsboy uses the same law in selling his newspapers, running a news-stand and climbing gradually to the mayoralty of his city or town. We all use this law of attraction no matter whether we know it or not. We use it every instant of our lives.

Many people wonder that bad men, wicked

men, vicious men are successful in business, at money making, in amassing a fortune, while the good man, the upright man, doesn't seem to be able to make any headway. They haven't the knack of accumulation in the way of making money. Good things do not seem to come to them. If they make an investment they almost always lose; they buy in the wrong market, or sell in the wrong market.

Now, a man's morals do not have anything specially to do with his money-making faculties, except that honesty is always and everywhere the best business policy. It is just a question of obeying the law of accumulation, the law that *like attracts like*. A very bad man may obey the law of accumulation, the law of attraction, and accumulate a vast fortune. If he is honest, his other defects and immoralities, his viciousness, will not hinder the working of the law. The law is unmoral —it is neither moral nor immoral.

Multitudes of people are attracting the wrong things because they do not know the law. They have never learned that the great secret of health, happiness, and success lies in holding the mental attitude which builds, which constructs, the mental attitude which draws to us the good things we desire. They have never learned the difference between building and tearing down thoughts; the difference between success and failure thoughts; in fact, they do not know that whatever comes to us in life, in our undertakings, great or small, is largely a question of the kind of thoughts we hold in the mind. We can attract the thing we desire as easily as we can attract the thing we hate and despise and long to get rid of. It is simply a matter of holding the image of the thing in the mind. That is the model which the life processes will build into our environment and which we will objectify.

Like attracts like, failure more failure, poverty more poverty. Hatred attracts more hatred, envy more envy, jealousy more jealousy, and malice more malice. Everything has power to attract its kind. The feeling of jealousy or hatred is a seed sown in the great cosmic soil all about us, and the eternal laws return to us a harvest the same in kind. What we sow we reap, just as the soil will return to us exactly what we put into it. Nothing has the power to reproduce anything but itself. There is no exception to this law.

The law cannot pity or help you if you break a bone or are injured, any more than the law of electricity can help you when you abuse it. It will kill you if you break the law.

To think about and worry about the things we do not want, or to fear that they will come to us, is but to invite them; because *every impression becomes an expression,* or tends to become so unless the impression is neutralized by its opposite. If we think too much about our losses, too much about our possible failure, all these things will tend to bring to us the very thing we are trying to get away from.

On every hand we see this law of like attracting like exemplified in the lives of the poverty-stricken multitudes, who, through ignorance of the law, keep themselves in their unfortunate condition by saturating their minds with the poverty idea; thinking and acting and talking poverty; living in the belief in its permanency; fearing, dreading, and worrying about it. They do not realize, no one has ever told them, that as long as people mentally see the hunger wolf at the door and the poorhouse ahead of them; as long as they expect nothing but lack and poverty and hard conditions, they are headed toward these things; they are making it impossible for prosperity to come in their direction. The way to attract prosperity and drive poverty out of the life is to work in harmony with the law instead of against it. To expect prosperity, to believe with all your heart, no matter how present conditions may seem to contradict, that you are going to become prosperous, that you are already so, is the very first condition of the law of attaining what you desire. You cannot get it by doubting or fearing. Whatever we visualize and work for we will get.

What we most frequently visualize, what we think most about, is constantly weaving itself into the fabric of our lives, becoming a part of ourselves, increasing the power of our mental magnet to attract those things to us. It doesn't matter whether they are things we fear and try to avoid or things that are good for us, that we long to get. Keeping them in mind increases our affinity for them and inevitably tends to bring them into our lives.

It is a curious fact that many people seem

to think that one must spend years as an apprentice to become an expert in any line of endeavor, in business or in a profession, but that in regard to prosperity it is largely a matter of chance, of fate, something which cannot be affected very much by anything they may be able to do.

They say, "Well, I was not built that way. I am not a natural money-maker, and never can be." Or they excuse themselves on the ground that their parents and those before them were never money-makers, and never did anything more than make a bare living.

There is nothing at all peculiar about prosperity any more than there is about legal efficiency or expertness in law or medicine. Its realization is purely a matter of concentration and of preparation; a matter of focusing all our powers upon the prosperity law in order to attract prosperity and to make ourselves expert in attaining it.

The law of prosperity, of opulence, is just as definite as the law of gravitation, and it works just as unerringly. Its first principle is mental. Wealth is created mentally first; it is thought out before it becomes a reality.

If you would attract success, keep your mind saturated with the success idea. Develop an attitude of mind that will attract success. When you think success, when you act it, when you live it, when you talk it, when it is in your bearing, then you are attracting it.

When we once get this law of attraction thoroughly fixed in our minds we will be careful about attracting our enemies, contacting with them through our mind, thinking about them, worrying about them, fearing, and dreading them. We will hold the sort of thoughts that will attract the things we long for and are seeking, not the things we dread, and despise, and are trying to avoid.

It is just as easy to attract what you want as to attract what you don't want. It is just a question of holding the right thought, and making the right effort. There is no exception to the law of attraction, any more than there is to the law of gravitation, or the laws of mathematics.

CHAPTER III

DRIVING AWAY PROSPERITY

As long as you hold the poorhouse thought you are heading toward the poorhouse. A pinched, stingy thought means a pinched, stingy supply.

The man who sows failure thoughts, poverty thoughts, can no more reap success, prosperity harvests, than a farmer can get a wheat crop from sowing thistles.

No matter how hard you may work, if you keep your mind saturated with poverty thoughts, poverty pictures, you are driving away the very thing you are pursuing.

Stop thinking trouble if you want to attract its opposite; stop thinking poverty if you wish to attract plenty. Refuse to have anything to do with the things you fear, the things you do not want.

It is doubting and facing the wrong way, facing towards the black, depressing, hopeless outlook that kills effort and paralyzes ambition.

A MAN once told me that if he could be assured that he would never have to go to the poorhouse, and that he would have the necessities of life for his family, he would be perfectly satisfied. He said it was evidently not intended that he should have luxuries or anything more than a bare living; he had always

23

been a poor man and he always expected to be poor, that his people before him had also been poor.

Now, it was just this mental attitude,—for he was a hard worker,—of always expecting to be poor, believing he would always be poor, that kept him from attracting prosperity. He had not expected prosperity and, of course, could not attract what he did not expect. He only just managed to get along, for that was all he expected to do.

One of the chief reasons why the great mass of human beings live such mean, stingy, poverty-stricken lives is because their negative mental attitudes, their doubts and fears and worries, their lack of faith, attract these conditions.

The Good Book tells us that "the destruction of the poor is their poverty." That is, their poverty thought, their poverty conviction, their poverty expectation and poverty belief, their general hopeless mental outlook keeps away prosperity. The worst thing about poverty is the poverty thought, the poverty belief.

Multitudes of people never expect to be

comfortable, to say nothing of having the luxuries and refinements of life. They expect poverty, and they do not understand that this very expectancy increases the power of their mental magnet to attract want and limitation, even though they are trying to get away from it; that we always head towards our expectations and convictions.

Poverty begins in the mind. The majority of poor people remain poor because they are mental paupers to begin with. They don't believe they are ever going to be prosperous. Fate, conditions are against them; they were born poor and they expect always to be poor, —that is their unvarying trend of thought, their fixed conviction. Go among the very poor in the slums and you will find them always talking poverty, bewailing their fate, their hard luck, the cruelty and injustice of society. They will tell you how they are ground down by the upper classes, kept down by their greedy employers, or by an unjust order of things which they can't change. They think of themselves as victims instead of victors, as conquered instead of conquerors.

The great trouble with most people who fail

to realize their ambition is that they face life the wrong way. They do not understand the tremendous potency of the influence of the habitual mental attitude in shaping the career and actually creating conditions.

It is really pitiful to see people making slaves of themselves trying to get ahead, but all the time side-tracking the good things which would come their way if they did not head them off by their conviction that there is nothing much in the world for them anyway, nothing more than a bare living at the best. They are actually driving away the very things which might flow to them in abundance if they held the right mental attitude.

In every walk of life we see men and women driving away the things they want. Most people think the things they do not want. They go through life trying to build happy, prosperous, healthful lives out of negative, destructive thinking, always neutralizing the results of their hard work. They indulge in worries, in fears and envies, in thoughts of hatred and revenge, and carry habitually a mental attitude which means destruction to health, growth, and creative possibility. Their lives are pitched to a minor key. There is always a downward tendency in their thought and conversation.

Nine-tenths of the people in the world who complain of being poor and failures are headed in the wrong direction, headed right away from the condition or thing they long for. What they need is to be turned about so that they will face their goal instead of turning their backs on it by their destructive thinking and going in the other direction.

The Morgans, the Wanamakers, the Marshall Fields, the Schwabs, think prosperity, and they get it. They don't anticipate poverty; they don't anticipate failure; they know they are going to be prosperous and successful, because they have eliminated all doubt from their minds.

Doubt is the factor which kills success, just as the fear of failure kills prosperity. Everything is mental first, whether failure or success. Everything passes through our consciousness before it is a reality.

Multitudes of people who work hard and try hard in every way to get on would be shocked if they could see a mental picture of themselves headed toward the poorhouse, in fact, as they actually are in thought. They do not know that, by an inexorable law, they must head toward their mental attitude, that when they continually think and talk poverty and suggest it by their slovenly dress, their personal appearance, and by their environment, when they predict that there is nothing for them but poverty, that they will always be poor, no matter how hard they may work. They do not know that their doubts and fears and poverty-stricken convictions are making prosperity impossible for them. They do not know that as long as they hold such thoughts they cannot possibly head toward the goal of prosperity.

The sum total of our life is that upon which we have concentrated. If poverty or opulence, if success or failure, if prosperity or want has occupied our minds, if we have focused our attention upon one of these, that is just what we shall see incorporated in our life.

What you have, my friend, what you have surrounded yourself with, is a reproduction of your thought, your faith, your belief in your efforts; is what you have been conscious of.

Our thoughts, our faith, our beliefs, our efforts, all materialize, and are objectified about us. Our words become flesh and live with us; our thoughts, our emotions, become flesh and live with us; they become our environment and surround us.

There is only one way to get away from poverty, and that is to turn your back upon it. Begin right away by putting the poverty thought, the poverty fear, out of your mind. Assume as far as possible a prosperous appearance; think the way you want to go; expect to get what you are after, the thing you long for, and you will get it.

Mentally and physically, in your clothing, in your surroundings, in your home, in your bearing, erase, as far as you can, all marks of poverty. Affirm with Walt Whitman, "I myself am good fortune." Don't let slovenliness in your home, shabbiness in your children or wife, be an unfavorable advertisement of you.

The fear of poverty is its greatest power. That is what gives it its stranglehold on the masses. Get rid of your fear of it, my friend. Let the prosperity thought take the place of the poverty thought, the poverty fear, in your mind. If you have been unfortunate, don't advertise your discouragement. Brush up, brace up, dress up, clean up; and above all— *look up and think up*. Give an uplook to your home, however humble.

Remember that a stream of plenty will not flow towards a poverty-saturated thought. A pinched, stingy thought means scanty supply. Thinking abundance, opulence, and defying limitations will open up the mind and set the thought currents towards greatly increased supply.

If all the poverty-stricken people in the world to-day would quit thinking poverty, quit dwelling on it, worrying about it and fearing it; if they would wipe the poverty thought out of their minds; if they would cut off mentally all relations with poverty and substitute the opulent thought, the prosperity thought, the mental attitude that faces toward prosperity, the change in their condition would be amazing.

The Creator never made a man to be poor. There is nothing in his constitution which fits drudgery and poverty. Man was made for prosperity, happiness, and success. He was not made to suffer any more than he was made to be insane or to be a criminal.

Thousands of people have literally thought themselves away from a life of poverty by getting a glimpse of that great fundamental principle—that we tend to realize in the life what we persistently hold in the thought and vigorously struggle toward.

Don't think that by holding the constructive, creative thought only now and then, or just when you may happen to feel like it, that it is going to counteract the influence of holding the destructive thought most of the time. Lots of people who treat for prosperity and opulence, hold the want thought, the lack thought too, and that is the reason their prayer is not answered. They get just the opposite, because that is the thought, the expectation which predominates in the mind.

Our conviction is much stronger than our will power. No will power can help you to do a thing when convinced that you can't. For instance, if you are convinced that a fatal disease which you believe you have inherited is overcoming you, this thought is infinitely stronger than your will to prevent it.

We cannot get away from our convictions. These are being built into the mind, being built into the life and character. If you are convinced that you are going to be poor, that you are never going to be prosperous, no matter how hard you may work, your convictions will triumph and you will live and die in penury. A man will never be anything but a beggar while he thinks beggarly thoughts.

If you are living in the thought of limitation, the conviction of lack and want, the fear of poverty, the belief that you can never become prosperous, you are holding yourself down, keeping yourself back. You are sowing seed which must produce a harvest like itself.

The boy who sows his wild oats seed might as well expect to get just the opposite harvest as for you to saturate your mind with poverty thoughts, lack, want, limitation thoughts, and expect a prosperity harvest. If you are thinking poverty-stricken thoughts, saturating your mind with limitation thoughts, you must expect a corresponding harvest and you will get it whether you expect it or not.

In my youth one of the hardest things in the Bible for me to understand was the statement, "To him that hath shall be given." I couldn't reconcile this with the Bible. It seemed positively unjust. But now I know that it illustrates a law. "To him that hath shall be given," because in getting what he has a man has made his mind a magnet to attract more. On the other hand, "To him that hath little, that which he hath shall be taken away," because he is headed in the wrong direction mentally. He is closing the avenues of supply by his little thoughts, his doubts and fears. He is in no mental condition to get more, to attract more.

If you want to demonstrate prosperity, you must think prosperity; you must hold your mind everlastingly toward prosperity; you must saturate your mind with it, just as a law student must saturate his mind with law, must think it, must read it, must talk it, must keep with lawyers and in a law atmosphere as much as possible, to be successful as a lawyer.

It was intended that we should have an abundance of the good things of the universe.

None of them are withheld from us except by our poverty-stricken mental attitude. There is no more possible lack for a human being of all that the heart can wish for than there is lack of water or food supply for the fish in the great ocean. The fish swims in the ocean of supply, as we swim in the great cosmic ocean of supply that is all around us. All we have to do is to open our minds, our faith, our confidence, to its reality, and use our intelligent effort to get all the good there is in it,—that is everything we need and desire.

CHAPTER IV

ESTABLISHING THE CREATIVE CONSCIOUSNESS

The beginning of every achievement must be in your consciousness.

We have unlimited power, boundless resources, in the great within of us, but until we awaken to a consciousness of this hidden power, those invisible resources, we cannot use them.

The consciousness of power creates power. What we are conscious of, we already possess.

In proportion to the intensity, the persistence, the vividness, the definiteness of your consciousness of the thing you want, do you begin to create it, to attract it.

The Creator puts no limit to our supply. There is no limitation of anything we need except in our own consciousness.

THE great trouble with those of us who are living in a world of unfulfilled desires and ambitions is that we do not hold the right consciousness. Dr. Perry Green rightly says that Job's lament—"The thing which I feared is come upon me"—should be changed to *"The thing which I was greatly conscious of is come upon me."* In other words, it is the thing we hold in our consciousness that comes out of

35

the invisible world of realities and takes visible form in our lives according to its nature,—poverty or prosperity; health or disease; happiness or misery.

The whole secret of individual growth and development is locked up in our consciousness, for this is the door of life itself. Every experience, whether of joy or sorrow, of health or disease, of success or failure, must come through our consciousness. There is no other way by which it can enter and become a part of the life. You cannot have what you are not conscious of; you cannot do what you are not conscious of being able to do. In short, it is an immutable law that, whatever you hold in mind, believe that you can do or get, is the thing that will manifest itself in your life. The thing that Job held in his consciousness was the thing that came upon him. Joan of Arc saved her country, because from childhood she held the consciousness that she had been born to do that very thing. This poor unlettered peasant girl knew nothing about the great law of mental attraction, but unconsciously she worked with it. But for her consciousness of victory she never could have accomplished her stupendous work.

It is the victorious consciousness that achieves victory in every age and in every field. After many years' study of the lives and methods of successful men in every department of life, I have found that those who win out in a large way are great believers in themselves, in their power to succeed in the things they undertake. Great artists, scientists, inventors, explorers, generals, business men, and others, who have done the biggest things in their specialty, have always held the victorious consciousness. Success was the goal they constantly visualized, and they never wavered in their conviction that they would reach it.

Men fail, not because of lack of ability, but because they do not hold the victorious consciousness, the success consciousness. They do not live in the expectancy of winning, in the belief that they will succeed in reaching the goal of their ambitions. They live rather in the expectation of possible failure, in fear of poverty, and coming to want, and they get what they hold in mind, what they habitually dwell upon. The pinched, narrow, limited, poverty-stricken, fear-filled consciousness; *the consciousness that expects stingy returns,* that expects poverty and does not believe it will get anything better, is responsible for more poverty than any other one thing.

Our consciousness is a part of our creative force; that is, it puts the mentality in a position to attract its affinity, that which is like itself. A penury consciousness cannot demonstrate a fortune; a failure consciousness cannot demonstrate success. It would be against the law. If you are steeped in poverty and failure, you have no one to blame but yourself, for you are working against the law. You are holding the poverty consciousness, living in the thought of failure. Perhaps you are wondering why you can't create something that will match your ambition, your longings when all the time you are filling your mind so full of discouragement, so full of black, gloomy, despairing pictures, that your whole life is saturated with the failure consciousness. You feel, perhaps, that something, some invisible force, some cruel fate or destiny is holding you back. Something is holding you back, but it is not fate or destiny; it is your discouraged mental attitude, the unfortunate consciousness that you have been holding for years. While you were trying to build on the material plane, you were neutralizing all your efforts by constantly tearing down on the mental plane. You have been obeying the negative law which destroys and kills, blights and blasts, instead of the positive law that produces; that creates, builds, beautifies, develops man's godlike qualities and glorifies his life.

All of life and its achievements, its possibilities, depend upon our consciousness, and we can develop any sort of consciousness we wish. The great musician has developed a musical consciousness of which most of us are ignorant, because we are not conscious of this mode of activity. Our musical consciousness has not been developed. The mathematician, the astronomer, the writer, the physician, the artist, the specialist in whatsoever line, has developed a particular consciousness, and he realizes the fruits of that consciousness. He manifests and enjoys a special power just in proportion as he has developed his specialty consciousness.

What sort of consciousness do you want to

develop? What do you want to get, to do, to become? Make yourself very positive on this point for the first step toward the development of a new consciousness is to get a thorough grip upon your purpose, your desire, your aim; to get a picture of it firmly fixed in your mind; to make it dominant in your thoughts, in your acts, in your life. This is how the successful lawyer at the start develops a law consciousness; the successful physician, a medical consciousness; the successful business man, a business consciousness. It is of the utmost importance to get started right, because whatever the consciousness you develop, your mind will attract that which has an affinity for it, will draw to you the material for your building.

The next thing is to establish the conviction that you can achieve whatever you desire. This is a tremendous step in the way of accomplishment, for conviction is stronger than will power. That is, you may will ever so hard to do a thing, but if you are convinced that you can't do it, the conviction of your inability will prevail over your will power. Your conviction is your strongest lever of accomplishment. This is what has enabled so many poor boys and girls to climb to high place and power in spite of all sorts of obstacles, and often contrary to the opinion and advice of those who knew them best. They were so thoroughly conscious of their ability to do the thing they wanted to do, and so convinced that they could do it, that nothing could hold them back from their own.

The beginning of every achievement must be in your consciousness. That is the starting point of your creative plan. In proportion to the intensity, the persistence, the vividness, the definiteness of your consciousness of the thing you want, do you begin to create in any line. For instance, consciousness of power reveals power; the consciousness of supremacy is equivalent to supremacy itself; the consciousness of self-confidence is what gives us the assurance that we are equal to the thing we undertake. What we are conscious of, we already possess. But we cannot come into possession of anything we are not conscious of. That is, it cannot be ours until we become conscious of it. If you are not conscious of the ability to succeed, you can't succeed. If you are not conscious of your own superiority, you cannot become superior. But if you hold in your consciousness the picture of masterfulness; if you hold in mind the thought of superiority, you are putting in operation a little law of mastership, a little law of superiority, and you begin to manifest these things in your life. We have unlimited power, boundless resources, in the great within of us, but until we awaken to a consciousness of this hidden power, those invisible resources, we cannot use them.

Some time ago a friend of mine saw a small, delicate woman leap over a six-bar gate when frightened by the sudden approach of a cow which she mistook for a bull. He said that this woman told him she could no more have done this under ordinary conditions than she could have lifted a corner of her house from its foundations. But she thought her life was in peril, and, in her great extremity, she became for a moment conscious of the power within. Seeing the cow running toward her, and imagining that it was an angry bull, she had no time to allow her doubts and fears as to whether she could leap over the gate to control her. It was the only means of escape in sight, and with the aroused consciousness of the latent power within her, she cleared the gate without difficulty. But when the imagined danger was past she lost the consciousness of her hidden strength and relapsed into her ordinary condition of weakness.

There are numerous instances on record where invalids and cripples, people who had been paralyzed for years, who did not feel that they could do anything whatever, have risen up from their beds when a fire or some terrible accident endangered their own lives or the lives of those dear to them, and then and there performed marvelous feats, in carrying heavy furniture out of a burning house, rescuing children, and doing other things that would have seemed miraculous even for strong men. Again and again unusual emergencies give us a fleeting consciousness of our vast reserve powers and we perform prodigies that amaze ourselves, but we don't continue to make the demand on them and the consciousness that it is possible for us to do anything out of the ordinary slips from us and our measureless resources remain untouched.

Emerson says: "Every soul is not only the inlet but may become the outlet of all that is in God." The consciousness of this great truth is the secret of all power. It is the full realization of our connection with Omnipotence, with Omniscience, with the Source of all there is, that enables us to use the vast powers that are within us, always at our command, waiting to accomplish our ends.

The Creator puts no limit to our supply. There is no limitation of anything we need except in our own consciousness. That is the door, which, according to its quality, shuts us off from, or admits us to, the great storehouse of infinite supply. The pinched, stingy consciousness never gets in touch with this supply. It is the man who has faith in his own power to meet whatever demands life may make upon him, who spends his last dollar fearlessly, because he knows the law of supply and is in touch with a flow of abundance, that gets on and up in the world. But the one who hoards his last dollar in fear and trembling, afraid to let go of it, even though he must go hungry, who always carries in his mind a vivid picture of the wolf at the door, never conquers poverty, because he never gets the prosperity consciousness.

A wonderful uplift and courage comes to the man who follows the aspiring tendency in his nature that bids him trust and look up, no matter how dark the outlook. Faith in the Power that orders all things well tells him that there is a silver lining to the black cloud which temporarily shuts out the light, and he goes serenely on, feeling confident that his plans will succeed, that his demands will be met. His is the consciousness that assures him, no matter what happens, that "God's in his Heaven; all's right with the world."

If you keep this one thing in mind, that we are always creating, always manifesting in our lives the conditions we hold in our consciousness, you will not make the mistake millions are making to-day, manifesting the things they don't want instead of the things they want. When we realize that our enjoyment, our happiness, our satisfaction, our achievement, our power, our personality, all depend on the nature of our consciousness, the aim and direction in which it is unfolding, we will not deliberately build up a consciousness of the very opposite of all that we are struggling to attain. On the contrary, we will hold constantly in mind the consciousness of our ambition, whatever it is, the consciousness of our heart's longings, our soul's desires; we will hold the truth consciousness, the God consciousness, the harmony consciousness, the opulent consciousness, and then we shall really begin to live. Then life will mean something more to all of us than it now does to most of us—a mere struggle for existence.

CHAPTER V

WHERE PROSPERITY BEGINS

Whatever we visualize intensely and persistently and back by intelligent effort we tend to create, vitalize into form, to build into the life.

It is in the unseen world that man, animated and inspired by the consciousness of his partnership with Divinity, is beginning to find some of the secrets of the universe,—lifting the race from animalism and drudgery, changing the face of the world, pushing civilization up to new and more glorious heights.

Limitless wealth, inexhaustible supply to meet our needs, undreamed of possibilities, are in the great cosmic intelligence waiting the contact of man's thought to bring them into visible form.

The invisible world about us is packed with infinite possibilities, awaiting our thought seed, our desire seed, our ambition seed, our aspiration seed, our prosperity and success seed, backed by our effort on the material plane, to make them manifest in the forms upon which we concentrate.

There is no lack of anything we need on God's earth any more than there is a lack of sunshine. Who would think of complaining that the sun refuses to shine on him, that its rays will not rest upon him, will not bring his crops to maturity, will not warm and cheer his life? There is no lack of sunshine, but we can cut ourselves off from it. If we choose to live in the shadows, if we go down into the dark cellar where the sun cannot enter, it is our own fault.

DURING his lecture tour in the United States, the great scientist, Sir Oliver Lodge, speaking on "The Reality of the Unseen," said: "Our senses are no criterion of existence. They were evolved for earthly reasons, not for purposes of philosophy, and if we refuse to go beyond the direct evidence of our senses we shall narrow our outlook on the universe to a hopeless and almost imbecile extent."

It is the most difficult thing in the world to convince people of the reality of anything they cannot perceive through the senses. Yet the realest things we know anything about are invisible; have never been seen by mortal eyes.

And right here lies the great difficulty for most people in changing undesirable conditions; in getting away from poverty and the things that are holding them back. They can't see beyond the present; they haven't learned to visualize the future, to see beyond the material things about them into the unseen world, packed with all creative energies, where the mind starts the creative processes. They do not realize that everything in the visible world that man has produced began in a mental vision; that the power of mind picturing, of visualizing the things we want to come into our lives, is God's priceless gift to man, to enable him to bring into visibility out of the invisible world whatever he wills.

Anyone who knows how to use this marvelous power can begin now to visualize his future; to see himself as he would like to be; to see himself mentally doing the things he would like to do; occupying the position he aspires to; and thus he will draw to himself the means necessary to build, step by step, in the material world the future as he sees it in his vision. By its aid we can bring ourselves out of a poverty-stricken, discordant environment into harmonious conditions, a harmonious environment, with the refinements and, if we will, the luxuries of life; or we may pervert it, and hold ourselves in degrading lack and poverty, limited, held back from self-development, the unfoldment of our possibilities, and all the joys of living.

Whatever we visualize intensely and persistently we create, vitalize into form, build into the life, bring into the actual. In other words, the vital substance from which man fashions circumstances, destiny, is in the unseen world where all potencies and power dwell. The very foundations of the universe and the things which are doing most for the world to-day are the unseen forces, eternal principles. The forces which transport us over the globe and bring its uttermost parts into instant communion; the power of the principles of chemistry, of gravitation, of cohesion, of adhesion,—all the mighty agencies operating in the universe and producing its phenomena,—we cannot see, hear, or touch, we cannot appreciate them with our senses only as we feel their effects; they are things we know little about, yet we know they are great realities.

Who knows or who has seen what is back of these great principles, these potencies which we know exist? Gravitation, which is holding the heavenly bodies in their orbits, which keeps the world so marvelously balanced in space, revolving at terrific speed around the sun, none of them varying in their revolutions in their orbits the fraction of a second in a thousand years, is an invisible force. Because we can't see or taste, or smell, or handle it, shall we say it is not a reality? That it does not exist?

We can see and feel the effects of electricity,

but who knows what this invisible force is? The Edisons, the Bells, the Marconis have, through experiments, found out certain things, certain laws governing it, through the operation of which we get heat, energy, and light. They have put it to work for us in a multitude of ways. It carries our messages under oceans and across continents. It has already done away with a large part of the drudgery of the world, and is destined to serve mankind in ways perhaps not yet dreamed of by even the wisest scientists and inventors. This mighty force which he has used in his thousands of inventions, Edison confesses he knows nothing about. He stands in awe of this mysterious power which has come out of the cosmic intelligence in response to his efforts. He regards himself merely as a channel through which some of its secrets have been passed along to man, to make life less toilsome, more comfortable, and more beautiful.

It is nonsense for skeptics and materialists to say that they take no stock in anything that they cannot test with their senses, when we know that the real force in the very things we live on, the elements that nourish and keep alive even the material part of us, are all invisible.

We cannot see the life-building, life-sustaining gases in the air we breathe; we cannot see the air, yet we take it into our body eighteen or twenty times a minute and get the silent, unseen power resident in it. The blood absorbs and sends it to the billions of cells in our bodies. None of its mysterious potency can we see or handle, yet we know we could not live a minute without it.

No one has ever seen the force in the food we eat, but we know it is there, that we get strength from it, and that after a time the apparently dead, inert matter comes to life in the body; that it acts, dreams, has experiences, works, creates.

Notwithstanding all its marvelous discoveries, science has not been able to uncover the secrets of the unseen forces everywhere at work in the universe. Who can see or explain the mystery of the unfolding bud, the expanding flower, the generating of the wonderful fragrance and marvelous beauty of the rose? Yet we know that there is reality back of them, an intelligence which plans and shapes them, brings them to their glorious maturity.

We know that all these things come from the same Omnipotent Source, that they are the creations of Divine Mind. Scientists are demonstrating that there is but one substance, one eternal force or essence, in the universe, and that all we see is a varying expression of it. To the senses this universal substance, which is the great reality back of all we see, is non-existent. We can neither see, nor touch, nor taste, nor smell it. Yet all the time science is piling up proof after proof that everything about us is merely a modification, a change of form, change of vibration of this universal substance, just as electricity is a manifestation of force in various forms.

We think we live in a material world, but in reality we live in a mental world, a world of externalized thought, a world controlled and guided by invisible forces. We contact with material things only at a few points in our lives. The corporal part of us is fed, warmed and clothed by material things, but we live, move, and have our being in the unseen.

When we come to the reality of ourselves, the soul, the spirit of man, which is one with God, we live altogether in an invisible world. The real self is the unseen self. The man whose reflection we see in the mirror is but the shadow of the reality. The material body of flesh and blood that we see, and can touch with our hands, is not the real man. That is behind what we see and touch. It is back of the cell, back of the atoms, back of the electrons which make up the body.

The new philosophy is going back of appearance and showing us the real man, the invisible man. It is revealing his hidden potencies and possibilities, and pointing the way to their development and use. It shows us that the impotent, sickly, ailing man, the weakling, the discouraged, disconsolate, complaining being, the failure, the man full of discord, disease, inharmony, is not the man God made; that this is the unreal creature man himself has made. This is the being that wrong thinking, wrong living, and unfortunate motives have made, the being who is the victim of his passions, of his moods, of his ignorance of realities, the great eternal verities of life.

We all learned as children that man is made in God's image and likeness, but the new philosophy urges us to act on this truth; to look beyond the appearance to the reality, to see with the inner eye the real man, the invisible man, who is one with his Creator. He is strong, vigorous, robust, with Godlike powers and qualities. He matches God's ideal of manhood. There is no suggestion of failure, of weakness, of instability, of sickness about him. He is perfect, immortal, unchangeable as truth itself, because the real man is the truth of being, changeless reality. No matter what his conditions or circumstances, the God stuff, the God principle, the divinity in him is still intact, still perfect, still contains all of his possibilities, is still stamped with nobility, with success, with health, with prosperity, with harmony, with the image of his Creator—for God's image and likeness is perfect, immortal.

If we could only realize this, and measure life with its infinite possibilities from the standpoint of the changeless reality of man, instead of from that of the changing unreality of the body; if we could only hold the thought that we are a part of the creative intelligence of the universe, copartners with God in our work here on the earth, how much more we could accomplish, how much higher we could climb, how much happier we should be!

When man realizes the tremendous significance of the reality of the unseen; when he grasps the truth of his unity with his Maker, the unity of life, the oneness of the source of all things in the universe, and that all is a manifestation of Divine Mind, he will come into possession of the illimitable power the Creator has implanted in every one of us.

When Christ emphasized the fact that the kingdom of heaven is within us, he meant that this kingdom within is identical with the Divine Mind, and that it is there man taps the source of all power, of all supply. The kingdom within is the kingdom of power, where all man's creative work is started. It is there he connects with the universal substance, the great creative energy; and thought is the invisible tool with which he fashions his creations. Acting upon the hidden, mysterious substance from which everything in the universe is evolved, the thought tool directs, controls, creates according to his desires. It finds its material in the unseen world, and in proportion as the mind grasps the reality of the unseen, the power and the possibilities are there. It is in the unseen world that man, animated and inspired by the consciousness of his partnership with Divinity, is beginning to find some of the secrets of the universe—lifting the race from animalism and drudgery, changing the face of the world, pushing civilization up to new and more glorious heights.

Your prosperity, your health, your happiness, your success, the fruition of your ambitions, all are in the great formless creative energy, ready to come into form when your thought does its part in starting the creative processes. Limitless wealth, inexhaustible supply to meet our needs, inventions, great productions of art and literature, music and drama, marvels in every field of human endeavor, are in the great cosmic intelligence waiting the contact of man's thought to come into visible form on our earth.

All the powers in the great cosmic intelligence are constantly working on the thoughts and desires of men. There is no favoritism in the unseen realities. The thoughts of the meanest man on earth are treated in precisely the same way as those of the noblest. Just as the sun and the rain, the wind and the dew give their potencies to the poor farmer and the good one alike, so the thief, the criminal, the murderer, the failure and the marplot have the same material to work in as the just man, the nobly successful, the great architects and artists, the great engineers, inventors, merchants, the great men and women in every field who are uplifting the race and making the world a better place to live in.

In other words, the creative force of thought puts an invincible power into man's hands, makes him a creator, the molder of his life, his destiny, his fortunes. We cannot think without creating, for every thought is a seed planted in the universal substance; it will produce something like itself. You and I can sow in the invisible, constructive thoughts, beautiful thoughts, thoughts of love, of good will, of health, of prosperity, of happiness, of success in our chosen work; or we can sow destructive thoughts, ugly thoughts, thoughts of hatred and ill-will, of disease, of discord, of failure, of poverty, of all sorts of misery, and, one thing is certain, whatever we sow we shall reap. That is the law, and there is no escape from it.

Most of the poverty, disease, failure and unhappiness in the world come from ignorance of the law. These things do not fit God's plan for his children. The Father never intended that we should be subject to disease, that we should wear ourselves out in drudgery, in unhappiness, in failure, in poverty, in constant anxiety, fearing all sorts of trouble and misery. The specter of disease and the wolf at the door are our own creations. They exist only in our minds; but as long as we visualize them, think on them, fear them, they will become real for us and manifest themselves in our lives.

Health, abundance, success, happiness, a glorious, joyful living—these are the things the Creator intended for all his children. But most of us drive them from us by our false, pessimistic thinking, and then whine and complain about "fate" and "hard luck," when just the reverse is true; when the invisible world about us is packed with infinite possibilities, awaiting our thought seed, our desire seed, our ambition seed, our aspiration seed, our prosperity and success seed, backed by our effort on the material plane, to make them manifest in the forms upon which we concentrate.

If you are poor, ailing and unsuccessful, you are working against the law, and until you come to a realization of the truth about the unseen forces at your command and work with the law you will continue to be poor, ailing, and unsuccessful.

Why not begin now to make the unseen forces your friends? Instead of making them your enemies, why not turn about face mentally and work with the law by simply holding the right thought? Why not turn your back on disease and poverty and failure by continually holding the health and abundance thought, saying to yourself: "I am the child of the Author of health, joy, and abundance; I am the child of the All-Supply. Health and success continually flow to me from the All-Supply, which is the Source of my being. Nothing but myself can cut me off from this Source; nothing but my own wrong thinking can cut off my supply,—the health, success, and happiness that are my birthright. I claim my inheritance from my Father now. I am health; I am success; I am happiness; I am free now and forever from all that would hinder my development, from everything that would hinder the realization of the ambitions the Father himself has implanted in me. This is my appointed work, the task he has given me to do here on this earth—to carry out the details of his plan for me is to realize my ambitions. I am working in partnership with Him and I cannot fail. I am one with Him; I again make my affirmation: I am health; I am success; I am happiness; I am abundance. My future is secure. I will go straight on, fearing nothing, for there is nothing to fear when I know that God is all, and that I am one with Him."

No matter what your present circumstances and environment, if you hold fast to this mental attitude, to a firm belief in the reality of the unseen, where your supply is, and work in harmony with the law, you can, through the creative power of thought, acting on the invisible universal substance, fashion and draw out of the unseen realms of supply whatever you will—knowledge, wisdom, power, health, wealth, happiness, success,—the realization of all your hopes and visions.

CHAPTER VI

IF YOU CAN FINANCE YOURSELF

Beware of little extravagances. A small leak will sink a big ship.—FRANKLIN.

Debt is like any other trap, easy enough to get into it, but hard enough to get out.—SHAW.

"The improvident man is a liability to the concern in which he is employed, the community in which he lives, his family and himself."

A little money in the bank is a great friend both in time of need and in time of opportunity.

Many people completely fail in life or are forced to live in mortifying poverty, to struggle along perhaps under the curse of debt, miserable, and handicapped all their lives because they never learned how to finance themselves.

THERE is nothing more important to a human being than to be able not only to earn his living, but also to know how to use his money to the best advantage, for on this depends his power to make himself independent and consequently to do his best work in the world.

The money sense, if not inherited, should be cultivated. Every child should be taught how to finance himself; he should know how to handle money, how to save money, how to spend it wisely for personal enlargement and for life enrichment.

Every child should be trained in thrifty habits, should learn the true value of money and should be able to feel the backaches in every dollar. If we do not teach our children to know what money means, how can we expect them to show wisdom in handling money in their maturity?

The average man does not use anything like the good judgment, the good sense in spending, in investing his money, that he does in earning it. A self-made millionaire tells me that not more than three men out of a hundred who have made money are able to hold on to it. Multitudes of men die without an independence, without a home, without even having been able to support themselves.

I am constantly running across men in middle life or later who have worked hard for many years and tried to get on; but they have nothing to show for it, have nothing laid by; they have no ready cash to enable them to avail themselves of opportunities and no good, solid investments. They have never made any headway since they were young men, because they never learned how to finance themselves. They are like the frog in the well, which keeps jumping up only to fall back again to the bottom from where it started.

There is no other one thing which will mean quite so much to you in after life, my young friend, as learning the art of handling money and knowing how to finance yourself wisely. If you cannot do this, you will always be an easy-mark for any smooth and oily promoter that happens along. Everybody will be aware of your gullibility and know that if you have any money it is not much of a trick to get it away from you.

Money is the slipperiest stuff in the world. The majority of people can't hold on to it any more than they could hold on to an eel or a greased pig. It slips through their fingers and disappears through all sorts of leaks of the pocketbook. Scores of men can make money where only one can hold on to it. There is always somebody who needs money, always some temptation to spend it.

Most people take too much risk with the money they have; they are too greedy, too anxious to keep it at work. They dislike to have a dollar on hand that is not earning something, and so they often make the most foolish investments.

There is one man of my acquaintance, an able business man in many respects, who has been in hot water most of his life because of this. He never has ready cash for any unusual opportunity or emergency. He is a fine chap, a popular man, and has much ability, but he cannot bear to keep money lying idle; it must be doing something; so he puts it into anything that offers, and then when good chances come he can't avail himself of them, because his money is tied up in some wildcat scheme. "Don't take chances with your little savings," is the advice of level-headed experts in financial matters.

Making foolish investments, trying to make large profits has kept vast multitudes of people in poverty all their lives. There is nothing like taking a stand in your early career only to invest in sound, solid, substantial things. The rich man can afford to take chances because if he loses he does not feel it, but you can't afford it. Go slow. The gambling instinct, the effort to make a fortune quickly, a lot of money with a little investment, is the cause of more unhappiness, of the poverty condition in more homes, than anything else I know of. It makes more disappointed lives, thwarts more ambitions, causes more people to die disappointed with their careers than any other thing.

One of the first steps in financing yourself properly is to keep a personal cash account. This is one of the best educators and teachers of economy and system. If the habit is formed when you are young in years it will never be broken. It will mean a competence in later life when otherwise there would have been none.

The world demands that every individual know how to take care of himself, how to be independent, self-reliant, how to finance himself wisely, how to make the most of his income.

However you make your living, whether by the work of your hand or of your brain, in a trade or in a profession, at home or in the shop, whether your income be small or large, you will always be placed at a disadvantage, unless you know how to finance yourself successfully. This is not to be "close," mean, or stingy, but to know how to make the most out of your income; not to expend the margin you should save in silly extravagances or to make foolish investments.

There is one thing that should be indelibly impressed upon every youth's mind, and that is the tragic consequences of debt, especially when incurred in early life. It has ruined many of the most promising careers. The youth should be so trained that under no consideration could he be induced to complicate his life by financial obligations. He should be shown that his success in life, the realizing of his ambition will depend very largely upon keeping his ability free from any sort of entanglement, and that he must keep this freedom at all costs. He should be taught that his unclouded enthusiasm and his zeal are very precious assets, and that nothing will kill these more effectively than the consciousness of being in a trap, the consciousness of being tied hand and foot by the curse of debt. The youth should be taught that to mortgage his future prospects would be fatal.

I have known quite a number of very promising young men to run in debt for automobiles. Many men have even mortgaged their little homes in order to get an automobile, trying to justify themselves by what it would mean to the health and pleasure of their wife and children.

Of course it would mean a lot to them, but, on the other hand, to a young man who is just starting out for himself, the purchasing of that which he cannot afford may handicap him for many years.

No one can be happy, no matter how optimistic, who is forever in the clutches of poverty, of harassing debt. I know a man who has literally lived in hades for many years because of early debts which he contracted when he had good credit. When he lost his business he had to struggle with this debt, until the interest doubled and trebled, and sometimes quadrupled. Nothing could have persuaded him to put his head in such a noose if he had realized what the result would be.

"To be broke is bad," says Dr. Frank Crane. "It's worse; it's a crime. It's still worse, for it's silly. Crimes can be pardoned and sins forgiven, but for the plumb fool there is no hope."

Now, the young man who puts nothing by for a rainy day or an emergency is a "plumb fool." And there are so many of them! As the late Marshall Field said, "the present-day tendency to live beyond their incomes brings disaster to thousands."

Many people live beyond their means because they cannot bear to have other people think that they cannot afford this and cannot afford that, that they cannot keep up appearances, their social standing. But it is better to be unpopular than to be embarrassed, better to be unpopular than to be in a hole, as someone suggests.

I AM—?

I am your best friend in time of need.

I can do for you what those who love you most are powerless to do without my aid.

I am the oil that smooths the troubled waters of life. I straighten out difficulties and remove obstacles that will yield to nothing else.

I am a supporter of faith, a spur to ambition, a tonic to aspiration, an invaluable aid to people who are struggling to make their dreams come true.

I give a man a fine sense of independence, a feeling of security in regard to the future, which increases his strength and ability and enables him to work with more vigor and spontaneity.

I am a stepping-stone to better things; a hope builder; an enemy of discouragement, because I take away one of the greatest causes of worry, anxiety, and fear.

I increase self-respect and self-confidence, and give a feeling of comfort and assurance that nothing else can give. I impart a consciousness of power that makes multitudes, who otherwise would cringe and crawl, hold up their heads and carry themselves with dignity.

I open the door to many opportunities for self-culture and to social and business advancement. I have enabled tens of thousands of young men, who made sacrifices to get me, to take advantage of splendid opportunities which those who did not have me were obliged to let go by.

I increase your importance in the world and your power to do good. I make people think well of your ability, increase their confidence in you; give you standing, capital, an assured position, influence, credit, and many of the good things of life that without me would be unattainable.

I am a shock-absorber for the jolts of life, a buffer between you and the rough knocks of the world. The man or woman who doesn't make an honest, determined effort to get me is lacking in one of the fundamental qualities that make for the happiness, the prosperity and well-being of the whole race.

Millions of mothers and children have suffered all sorts of hardships and humiliations because husbands and fathers lacked this practical quality, which would have saved themselves and those dependent on them so much suffering and misery.

Multitudes have spent their declining years in homeless wretchedness, or eked out a miserable existence in humiliating dependence on the grudging charity of relatives, while other multitudes have died in the poorhouse, because they failed to make friends with me in their youth.

I am one of the most reliable aids in the battle of life, the struggle for independence; ever ready to help you in an emergency—sickness in your family, accident or loss, a crisis in your business—whatever it may be. You can always rely on me to step into the breach and do my work quietly, effectively, without bluster.

I AM—A LITTLE READY CASH

CHAPTER VII

HOW TO INCREASE YOUR ABILITY

Our ability is as sensitive to our moods, our feelings, our mental attitudes, as the mercury is to the changes of the weather or a weather-vane is to the currents of air.

The perpetual taunting and haunting of unsatisfied ambition, the consciousness that one has the ability to do the bigger thing, but is obliged to do the lesser because one did not early in life persist in following the path that led to the bigger; to feel cramped and limited in a little seven-by-nine situation in middle life or later, when one knows that he has the natural ability to fill an infinitely bigger place, is a hell on earth.

Hope, self-confidence, assurance, faith in one's mission, enthusiasm in one's work, optimism, courage, joy, open up the ability accordion wonderfully. Fear, anger, envy, prejudice, jealousy, worry, smallness, meanness, selfishness, close it.

Happiness in our work, the consciousness that we are doing our best, looking our best, and making a good impression on others—these are tremendous enlargers of ability, because they increase one's self-respect and self-appreciation. They give one assurance, confidence, and confidence gives a marvelous impetus to initiative and executive ability.

A PROMINENT business man says that the best contract he ever got was one he lost.

Why? Because it set him to investigating the cause of the loss, to investigating himself, to finding the weak places in himself and in

74

his business methods. It was the lost contract that led him to the discovery that he was not using more than half the ability he actually possessed.

Most people rob themselves of success and fortune by mistaken ideas about their ability. They are like a young stenographer who told me that if she had the ability to become an expert in her line, she would go to evening school, study nights, and do everything she could to improve her education and to develop herself in all possible ways. But as she was sure that she had only a very moderate share of ability, she was convinced that there was no use in trying, and that she must be satisfied with an ordinary position. In other words, she believed that her ability was a fixed quantity; something which could not be enlarged or diminished, which she could not change in any respect any more than she could change the color of her hair or of her eyes.

Now, the idea that our ability is an invariable quantity, fixed by heredity, or by some immutable law which we can neither understand nor control, is one of the most unfortunate that could take possession of anyone's mind. And nothing could be farther from the truth, for, as a matter of fact, human ability is a very variable and a very elastic quantity. It can be expanded almost indefinitely, or contracted, in a great many ways. It is like an accordion, which the player sometimes draws out to its full extent, and again closes completely. For instance, you can close up your accordion by wrong thinking until but a mere fraction of your possible ability is available, or you can open it up by right thinking and make every bit of it count in making your work, your life, a grand success.

Multitudes of people go through life with their actual ability so cramped, so muzzled and suffocated by their negative, destructive mental attitude, their doubts, fears, worries, superstitions and preconceived ideas, their lack of courage, their lack of faith in themselves and in their mission, that they make but a very small percentage of it count in their life work, even when they make a supreme effort to do so. Everywhere we see men and women, hard workers, who do not accomplish a tithe of what they could accomplish, with half the effort and half the time they now expend, if they would only keep their minds in a positive, creative condition, and face life in the right way.

While the development and sharpening of the different mental faculties is the first essential to the increase of our natural ability, it is a mistake to think that all of our ability expansion is dependent on this. It doesn't matter what amount of natural ability you have, if it is unavailable, bottled up by your pessimism, your doubts, your fears, your cowardice and lack of faith, it is useless to you. If you had a valuable gold mine on your property, and, instead of clearing away all obstructions to get at the ore you should add a lot more, your gold mine wouldn't add one particle to your available wealth. Potentially you had an immense fortune, but so far as you were concerned it might just as well not be there, for you derived no benefit from gold you could not get at and exchange for the good things of life that you desired. It is just the same with your ability. If instead of doing everything in your power to make it available, to give it outlet, you shut it up within you, covering it over with all sorts of mental obstructions, it will never expand, will never yield you anything.

Many of us think if we only had some other person's talent or opportunities; if we only had the advantages of some other fellows near us; if only we were superbly equipped with facilities for our particular work, that we would do wonderful things. Now, the Creator never sent anyone into this world without equipping him with just the tools required for the job He meant him to do, the job which He qualified him in every respect to do. He didn't sharpen the tools for us, because if He had done that He would have deprived us of the very thing that is designed for our expansion and growth. It is by drawing out all that is in us, by bettering our work each day, by overcoming obstacles, clearing away the rubbish and mental débris that choke our growth, and always reaching up to the attainment of our highest ideal, that, day by day, we unfold layer after layer of the wealth of ability that is enfolded in every human being, no matter what his apparent disabilities or handicaps.

Helen Keller is, perhaps, one of the most remarkable examples the world has ever seen of the power of the determined soul to overcome everything that stands in the way of its complete development. Deaf, dumb, and blind at the age of eighteen months, what opportunity was there for a human being so handicapped to do anything of value in the world; to become anything other than a despair to herself, a hopeless, helpless burden on her relatives? Yet out of her world of darkness the indomitable spirit within evolved a being of such remarkable ability and power that there are few to-day who are rendering greater service to humanity than this woman who, apparently, at the outset of life was hopelessly handicapped. She is a wonderful illustration of the truth that there is no limit to man's development, and no insuperable obstacles to his development except those he himself puts in his way.

The eagle is the mightiest and most powerful of all the feathered tribe. It can fly higher and remain longer on the wing than any other bird. Yet if this monarch of the air were held captive, tied by one of its feet to a huge ball or heavy weight, it could not fly as high as a barn-yard fowl. No matter how strong its natural instincts to soar into the heavens, it could not move from the earth.

Now, like the eagle, man was made to fly high, to do great things, but multitudes of people spend their lives doing little things instead of the big things they are capable of doing because of something which chains their ability and holds them down in an inferior position. There is a vast amount of unproductive ability in the great failure army to-day, which was never given an opportunity to fulfill the purposes for which the Creator meant it. Some of the most pitiable instances of spoiled lives I know of are those of men and women of middle age who really have the ability to do something large and grand, but who have failed to do so because of their unwillingness to make sacrifices in youth for the sake of their ambition. Love of ease enchained their faculties and held them prisoners until their ambition died and they lost even their desire to fly.

Some people are tied down by bad physical or mental habits, which make it impossible for them to put their best selves into their work.

There is a constant leakage of energy and vital force, resulting from preventable causes, which hinders their progress at every step and makes their ability unavailable. Others are held down by character traits or peculiarities of disposition which handicap all their success qualities and neutralize their efforts to advance. A quick temper, a jealous, envious disposition, lack of faith and self-confidence, vacillation, bashfulness, timidity, carelessness, inaccuracy and a host of other faults and weaknesses seriously hamper the development of their ability and act like weights in holding them down when they are eager to go up higher.

Whatever causes inharmony in the mind robs us of power and hinders our advancement. If you would gain control of all your resources and increase your ability, avoid as you would poison everything that tends to make you negative,—worry, anxiety, jealousy, envy, fear, cowardice, the whole family of depressing, despondent thoughts. They are all confessions of weakness, and may be summed up as power destroyers. Every fit of the blues, every unhappy thought, every feeling of discouragement, of despondency, every doubt, every fear, is a crippler of ability. In other words, our ability is extremely sensitive to our moods, to our mental condition generally. When we don't feel like it, when we are out of sorts, when for one reason or another we feel blue, discouraged, despondent, full of doubt and anxiety, our ability is very much contracted. On the other hand, when we are in good trim, when our minds are harmonious, not anxious or worried about anything, it is enormously expanded. That is, all the positive, uplifting, encouraging, cheerful emotions and feelings expand or increase our ability, while all of the negative, depressing, discouraging, gloomy ones contract or lessen it.

This shows that after we have done everything in our power to increase our ability by education, by training for our special work, by sharpening and improving our natural gifts and faculties in every possible way, we can yet so contract or expand it by our mental attitude, that it is safe to say nine-tenths of its availability depends upon our state of mind at any given time. We all know how it is enlarged by a sublime self-confidence, an unwavering faith, and how it is contracted by the lack of faith in ourselves, by self-depreciation, by timidity, and lack of courage. You know how much bigger a man you are, how much more capable of planning and doing things, when your courage is up and you believe in yourself, than when you are blue and discouraged. You know from experience that your consciousness of ability expands so you feel as though you could tackle almost anything. Make this your habitual state of mind and your ability will always be available, always at its maximum.

On the other hand, hold a poor opinion of yourself, refuse to assume responsibility, always berate yourself and belittle your powers, and if you had the natural ability of a Plato you would never amount to anything. This sort of mental attitude holds down more real ability, keeps more deserving merit in mediocre positions, than perhaps any other handicap in the gamut of human disabilities. Multitudes who have excellent mental endowments and splendid traits of character remain practically nobodies all their lives because of timidity, a sense of inferiority, a doubting, self-depreciating attitude toward themselves. Others with half their natural ability forge ahead, make fortunes, attain places of power and influence, while they remain in poverty and obscurity.

Everywhere in life the timid, retiring, self-effacing man is placed at a tremendous disadvantage, mentally, socially and in a business and professional way. People may be sorry for him, they may pity him, and his friends may say he has great ability and splendid traits of character; but this is not enough. Lacking self-confidence, push, assurance, the courage to demonstrate his ability to the world, he will not win out in anything in a large way. His mean opinion of himself will neutralize a large percentage of his real ability.

Every man has more ability than he thinks he has, more than he ever uses ordinarily. Under the impulse of a strong motive, a new stimulus to exertion, or having a great responsibility thrust upon us, being put in a situation where we must either sink or swim, there isn't one among us that wouldn't respond to the demand and unfold an amount of ability which we never before dreamed we possessed.

Some men's ability lies so deep that they are never at their best except in a great crisis. Then the giant in them is unshackled, and great powers, of which they themselves were ignorant, are unlocked within them.

Responsibility is a great ability developer. We often see a good example of this when a young man is taken into partnership in a large concern. His initiative, his executive force, his courage, all the ability-expanding qualities, are so strengthened by the stimulus of promotion that he goes ahead and does things that he did not dream he could ever accomplish when he was an employee. Now, taking him into partnership did not add to his latent ability at all, but it gave him more confidence in himself, and the fact that he is put on his mettle to make good in the new position compels him to draw on his ability to the limit, and he does make good. Never side-step a responsibility. It is throwing away an opportunity to enlarge your ability.

If an Edison should invent an instrument by means of which it would be possible for men and women to increase their natural ability fifty per cent. there is no price we would not be willing to pay for such an instrument. Yet there isn't a man or woman, a boy or girl, living to-day who can't do this by right thinking, facing life the right way, and using the opportunities that are at hand. Right where you are, no matter what your environment, what your disadvantages or handicaps, you have enough ability to make you a success in whatever you desire to do; to lift you out of lack and poverty and make you a millionaire. Expand your ability; do everything that will enable you to stretch your accordion to its limit, and you will be amazed at what you can accomplish.

CHAPTER VIII

LOOK LIKE A SUCCESS

You have no more right to go about among your fellows with a vinegar expression on your face, radiating mental poison, spreading the germs of doubt, fear, discouragement and despondency among them, than you have to inflict bodily injuries on them.

To be a conqueror in appearance, in one's bearing, is the first step toward success.

Walk, talk, and act as though you were a somebody, and you are much more likely to become such.

Let victory speak from your face and express itself in your manner, your conversation, your bearing.

Never show the world a gloomy, pessimistic face, which is an admission that life has been a disappointment to you instead of a glorious triumph.

When a man feels like a king he will look kingly. Majesty more regal than ever sat on a throne will look out of his face when he has learned how to claim and express the divinity of his birthright.

WHEN Frank A. Vanderlip, former president of the National City Bank, New York, was a reporter on the Chicago "Tribune," he asked his chief to tell him what he thought would be the greatest help to a man struggling to succeed. *"Look as if you had already succeeded,"* was the prompt reply.

This made a great impression upon young Vanderlip and completely changed some of his ideas on the subject, especially in regard to dress. From that time he began to spruce up, to be more particular about his general appearance. His chief had opened his eyes to the great value of appearances, especially in making a first impression. He became convinced that if a man did not look prosperous, people would think he did not have the right ambition or the ability to succeed; that there must be something the matter with him or he would dress better and make a better appearance.

Charles W. Eliot, President-emeritus of Harvard, said that much of one's success would depend on others' opinion of him, of those to whom he, perhaps, had never spoken a word, had never even seen. One's reputation travels by various routes in every direction and, according to its nature, will have a big influence on one's career.

It is a great thing to form a habit of going through the world giving the impression to everybody that you are a winner, that you are bound to be somebody—to stand for something worth while in the world. Let this idea stand out in everything you do, in your conversation, your appearance. Let everything about you make the world say, "He is a winner; keep your eye on him."

If you are anxious to win out in a large way, cultivate the bearing of success, the appearance of a successful man. If you carry about with you a defeated, poorhouse atmosphere; if your appearance suggests slovenliness, slipshodness, the lack of system and order, the lack of energy, of push, of the progressive spirit, you can't expect others to think you are an efficient, up-to-date person, pushing to the front.

Of course every employer knows that it sometimes happens that a shabbily dressed man, with baggy trousers and soiled linen, may have a lot of good stuff in him, but they don't expect it. The chances of finding a very valuable employee with such an advertisement of himself is so small that most men won't take the risk.

Your dress, your bearing, your conversation, your conduct, should all square with your ambition. All of these things are aids to your achievement, and you cannot afford to ignore any one of them. The world takes you at your own valuation. If you assume the victorious attitude toward it, it will give you the right of way.

One reason why it is so difficult for many young people to get a start, to get on, comes from the fact that they do not create in others the impression of power, of the force that achieves, that does things. They do not realize how much their reputation has to do with their getting on in the world. They do not realize that other people's confidence is a tremendous force.

A great physician or lawyer gets his reputation largely from the impression which he makes upon people, not only in the way he performs the duties of his profession, but also in his general attitude.

We weigh, measure, and estimate people by the impression they make upon us, everything considered. The victorious attitude inspires confidence in others as well as in oneself. Its psychological effect is compelling. Walk, talk,

and act as though you were already the man
you long to be, and you are unconsciously putting into operation unseen forces that bend circumstances to the accomplishment of your will.

Let your air be that of a winner, of a man
who is resolved to make his way in the world—
to make himself stand for something. Put
energy and life into your step; vim, force, vitality, pep into every movement of your
body. Look straight forward; never wince.
Don't apologize for taking up room on the
earth which might be filled to better advantage by another; you have just as much right
here as any other human being, if you are making good, and if you are not making good
you should be.

No matter what comes to you, defeat, threat-
ened failure, never lose your victorious consciousness. Let people read this declaration in
your bearing, in your life generally: "I am
a winner; I have not shown the white feather.
I have not shirked; I have done my part; I
have not been a sneak; I have not been a thief
or a cheat, wearing and using what others have
earned and giving nothing back in return. I

have done my part and can hold up my head and look the world in the face!"

The more trying your situation, the harder the way looks to you, the darker the outlook, the more necessary it is to carry that victorious consciousness. If you carry the down-and-out expression, if you confess by your very face that you are beaten, or that you expect to be, you are a goner. The victorious idea of life, not the failure idea; the triumphant, not the thwarted, ambition is the thing to keep ever uppermost in the mind, for it is this that will lead you to the goal you aspire to reach.

Have faith in your God-given power to succeed in a worthy ambition. Concentrate your efforts on its realization, and nothing on earth can keep you back from success. Such a mental attitude will make you a winner from the start, because you always head toward your thought, toward your conviction of yourself. The conviction that you are born to win is a tremendous creative force in your life, just as the conviction that you are a failure will keep you down till you change the model of yourself. Life is not a losing game. It is always victorious when properly played. It is the players who are at fault.

God did not make a man to be a failure. He made him to be a glorious success. The great trouble with all failures is that they were not started right. It was not drilled into the very texture of their being in youth that what they would get out of life must be created mentally first, and that inside the man, inside the woman, is where the great creative processes of all that we realize in our careers are carried on. Most of us depend too much upon the , things outside of us, upon other people, when the mainspring of life, the power that moves the world of men and things, is within us.

Think what it would mean to the world to-day if all the people who look upon themselves as nobodies and failures, dwarfs of what they might have been and ought to be, would get this triumphant idea of life into them! If they could once get a glimpse of their own possibilities, and would assume the victorious, the triumphant, attitude, they would revolutionize the world.

How many people form the chronic habit of indulging in frequent fits of depression!

They allow the "blues" an easy entrance to
their minds, in fact, are always at home to
them, and are susceptible to every form of discouragement that comes along. Every little
setback, every little difficulty, sends them into
the "blues" and they will say "What's the use!"
As a result their work is poor and ineffective,
and they do not attract the things they desire.

Every time you give way to discouragement,
every time you are blue, you are going backward, your destructive thoughts are tearing
down what you have been trying to build. One
fit of discouragement, visualizing failure or
poverty-stricken conditions, will rapidly destroy the result of much triumphant thought
building. Your creative forces will harmonize
with your thoughts, your emotions and moods;
they will create in sympathy with them.

Saturate your mind with hope, the expectation of better things, with the belief that your
dreams are coming true. Be convinced that
you are going to win out; let your mind rest
with success thoughts. Don't let the enemies
of your success and happiness dominate in your
mind or they will bring to you the condition
that they represent. Destroy the thoughts

and emotions and convictions which tend to destroy your hope, your ambitions, to tear down the results of your past building. If you don't they will create more failure, more poverty. If you want to realize success, think creative, successful conditions.

Set your character and your whole life towards triumph, towards victory. Hold the victorious thought towards yourself, towards your future, towards your career; it will tend to create the conditions favorable to the carrying out of your ambition, the fulfilling of your desires.

"Go boldly, go serenely, go augustly;
Who can withstand thee then!"

I know of nothing that gives more satisfaction than the consciousness that we have formed the habit of winning, the habit of victory, the habit of carrying a victorious mental attitude, of walking, acting, talking, looking like a winner, a conqueror. That sort of attitude always keeps the dominant, helpful qualities in the fore, always in the ascendancy.

One of the most obstinate habits to overcome in mature life, and one fatal to efficiency, is the habit of being defeated. Never allow yourself to fall into it. You may learn a lesson from every defeat that will make a new stepping-stone to your ambition.

Success is every human being's normal condition; he was made for success; he is a success machine, and to be a failure is to pervert the intention of his Creator. Every youth should be taught to assume a triumphant attitude towards life, to carry himself like a winner, because he was made to win. No child is really educated until he has learned to live a victorious life. That is what real education spells, victory. The habit of winning out in whatever we undertake can be formed almost as easily as the habit of being defeated, and every victory helps us to win other victories.

From the cradle a child should be taught that he is divine, a god in the making, and that he should hold up his head and go forth with confidence, because he is destined for something superb. Teach the child that he came to the earth with a message for mankind, and that he should deliver it like an ambassador. Show him that wrestling with difficulties is like practicing in a gymnasium where every victory over his muscles makes him so much stronger, and makes the next attempt so much surer and easier. Let him fully understand that every problem solved in school, every errand promptly and courteously performed, every piece of work superbly done, is just so much more added to his winning power, to the strength of his success possibilities.

The great prizes of life are for the courageous, the dauntless, the self-confident. The man who is timid and hesitating, who stops to listen to his fears, lets many a good opportunity pass beyond his reach.

If you find you are inclined to be timid; if you lack courage and initiative; if you are too bashful to speak or express your opinions when it is desired; if you blush, and stammer, and are awkward when you would appear calm and self-possessed, you can overcome your defects and build up the qualities you lack by training your subjective self to be courageous, unembarrassed, at your ease in any surroundings. Constantly suggest courage and heroism to this inner self. Stoutly deny that you are timid, cowardly, afraid to speak or to be natural in public or before anyone. Assert that you are brave, that you are not afraid to do anything that it is right and proper you should do.

Practice walking about among your fellows as though you were brave, courageous, self-confident, perfectly sure of yourself, as capable of carrying on a conversation creditably, or of entering a room gracefully as you are of discharging your daily duties.

Hold the triumphant thought towards your future, towards your ideal, your dream. Carry the atmosphere of the victor. Learn to radiate power. Let everything about you bespeak confidence, strength, masterfulness, victory. Let everybody who has anything to do with you see that you are a born winner.

You must not go about as though life had been a disappointment, as though you had no special ambition in life. If you want to stand for anything unusual; if you want to carry weight in the world; if you want to make your neighbors proud that you live near them, you must brace up in every respect. Keep yourself up to standard. Don't go about like a failure, like a nobody. Don't go about in a sloppy, slovenly way. Dress up, brace up, look up, struggle up. Let the world see, as you walk about, that you think well of yourself, and that there is a reason for it. Let people see that you are conscious you are on a superb mission, playing a superb part in the great life game. You will soon begin to see the thing you are looking for instead of the thing you are afraid of, and will find your dreams coming true.

CHAPTER IX

HOW TO MAKE YOUR DREAMS COME TRUE

Our heart longings, our soul aspirations are prophecies, predictions, forerunners of realities. They are indicators of our possibilities, of the things we can accomplish.

The moment you resolve to make your life dream come true, you have taken the first step towards its realization, but you will stop there if your efforts cease.

Keeping right after your ideals, nursing your visions, cultivating your dreams, visualizing the thing you long for vividly, intensely, and striving with all your might to match it with reality—this is what makes life count.

Our dreaming capacity gives us a peep into the glorious realities that await us further on.

> Dreams are true while they last,
> And do not we live in dreams?
> TENNYSON.

WHEN Gordon H. Selfridge, former manager of the Marshall Field Company, went to London and there established a great department store of the Marshall Field type, he only took the final step in the realization of a dream which he had nursed for years. Long before he stepped foot on the shores of England, he had had the department store all worked out in his mind. He had built it mentally before he crossed the Atlantic, and already in his mind's eye, saw it a marvelous success. "I pictured the great crowds of customers headed toward my new store," he said, "and could see it full of eager buyers long before I went to England."

From the time that the idea of a department store in London took form in his mind, Mr. Selfridge kept visualizing the completed structure. He kept his dream alive and vivid by the determination to make it come true. He would not allow it to be shattered, or let his idea be driven out by doubts, fears, and uncertainties, or by the well meant advice of his friends: to keep out of England because the English people were so slow to new ideas that he would fail if he went there. He didn't heed what they said, for he didn't believe that the English people were so unprogressive as they thought. He believed that they would respond to the American idea, the Marshall Field idea, and that the methods which had proved so successful in the United States would also be successful in England.

The amazing popularity of the Selfridge Department Store, which has long been one of the sights of London, is but another proof that the dreamer who dreams dreams and sees visions is always wiser than, and always ahead of, the so-called practical, wise ones who discourage him and try to turn him aside from his vision. The men and women who, in all ages, have done great things in the world have always been dreamers, have always seen visions, and always pictured their dreams as realities; visualized themselves accomplishing the things they were ambitious to do long before they were able to work them out in the actual and make them realities.

Columbus, Stephenson, Charles Goodyear, Elias Howe, Robert Fulton, Cyrus W. Field, Edison, Bell—all the great discoverers, scientists, explorers, philanthropists, inventors, philosophers, who have pushed the world forward and done immeasurable service to mankind, have visualized their dreams, nursed their visions through long years, many of them in the midst of poverty, persecution, ridicule, opposition, and contumely of all sorts, until they brought their dreams to earth and made them realities.

In making a study of the methods of successful men and women I have found that they are almost invariably strong and vivid visualizers of the things they are trying to accomplish. They are intense workers as well as dreamers, and nurse their vision tenaciously until they match it with reality. They build castles in the air, but they put the solid foundation of reality under them.

When Lillian Nordica was a poor girl, singing in the little church choir in her native village in Maine, when even her own people thought it a disgrace for a girl to appear on the stage, to sing in public concerts or in opera, she was picturing herself a great prima donna singing before vast audiences in her own country, in foreign capitals, and before the crowned heads of Europe.

When young Henry Clay was practicing oratory before the domestic animals in a Virginia barn and barn-yard, he visualized himself swaying vast audiences by his eloquence. When Washington was a lad of twelve he pictured himself as a leader, rich and powerful, a man of vast importance in the life of the colonies, and the ruler of a nation he would help to create.

When the young John Wanamaker was delivering clothing in a pushcart in Philadelphia, he saw himself as the proprietor of a much larger establishment than any then in that city. He saw beyond that and glimpsed the Wanamaker of later days, the great powerful merchant, with immense stores in the world's leading capitals.

Young Carnegie pictured himself a powerful figure in the steel world, as did the youth Charles M. Schwab, even when an ordinary employee. When working at the Homestead plant Schwab told Mr. Carnegie what he wanted was not more salary, not a larger position as a mere employee; that his ambition was to be a partner in the concern. That was the only thing that would satisfy him.

Now this sort of visualizing is not mere vanity, or petty egotism, it is the God urge in men pushing them out beyond themselves, beyond what is visible to the physical eye, to better things. The Scriptures tell us that without a vision the people perish. I have never known a man to do anything out of the common, who was never able to see beyond the visible into the vast invisible universe of the things that might be; who did not keep clearly in his mind the vision of the particular thing he was trying to accomplish.

It is the man who can visualize what does not yet exist in the visible world about us and see it as a reality; the man who can see thriving industries where others see no chance, no opportunities; the man who sees teeming cities, great populations on the prairies where others see only sagebrush, alkali plains, desolation; the man who sees power, opulence, plenty, success, where others see only failure, limitation, poverty, and wretchedness, who eventually pushes to the top and wins out.

It was this sort of vision that made James J. Hill the great "empire builder" of the Northwest. His dream of a great system of railroads that would cause millions of fertile farms to spring up along their route and make the desert blossom like a rose, was laughed at as a visionary scheme by many of those who were working for him when he died. They were men who had never been able to make a place and a name for themselves, because they had never learned that the great secret of success lies in visualizing dreams and making them come true. Perhaps they did not believe in their dreams, and put them out of their minds as mere idle fancies.

Many people seem to think that the imagination, or visualizing faculty, is a sort of appendix to the brain, that it is not a fundamental or necessary part of man, and they have never taken it very seriously. But those of us who have studied mental laws know that it is one of the most important functions of the mind. We are beginning to discover that the power to visualize is a sort of advance courier, making announcement of the things that the Creator has qualified us to bring about. In other words, we are beginning to see that our visions are prophecies of our future; mental picture programs, which we are supposed to carry out, to make concrete realities.

For instance, a youth whose bent is entirely in another direction is not haunted by an architectural vision, an art vision, a mercantile vision, or a vision of some other calling for which he has no natural affinity. A girl does not dream of a musical career for years before she has the slightest opportunity for taking up music as a career if she has no musical talent, or if her ability in some other line is much more pronounced. Boys and girls, men and women, are not haunted by dreams to do what nature has not fitted them for. We dream a particular dream, see a particular vision, because we have the talent and the special ability to bring the dream, the vision, into reality. Of course, I do not mean by dreams and visions the mere fantasies, the vague, undefined thoughts that flit through the mind, but our real heart longings, our soul yearnings, the mental pictures of a future which haunts our dreams, and the insistent urge which prods us until we try to match them with their reality, to bring them out into the actual. There is a divinity back of these visions. They are prophecies of our possible future; and nature is throwing up these pictures on our mental screen to give us a glimpse of the possibilities that are awaiting us.

One reason why most of us do such little, unoriginal things is because we do not sufficiently nurse our visions and longings. The plan of the building must come before the building. We climb by the ladder of our visions, our dreams. The sculptor's model must live in his own mind before he can call it out of the marble. We do not half realize the mental force we generate by persistently visualizing our ideal, by the perpetual clinging to our dreams, the vision of the thing we long to do or to be. We do not know that nursing our desires makes the mental pictures sharper, more clean cut, and that these mental processes are completing the plans of our future life building, filling in the outlines and details, and drawing to us out of the invisible energy of the universe the materials for our actual building.

There is no other one thing you will find so helpful in the attainment of your ambition as the habit of visualizing what you are trying to accomplish, visualizing it vividly, just as distinctly, just as vigorously as possible, because this makes a magnet of the mind to attract what one is after. All about us we see young men focusing their minds with intensity and persistence on their special aims and attracting to themselves marvelous results. A medical student holds in his mind a vision of himself as a great physician or surgeon, and in a few years we are amazed at the size of his practice. He called it out of the great universal supply by his perpetual visualizing, the constant intensifying of his desire, and the unceasing struggle on the material plan to make his dream come true.

Even if you are only a humble employee, visualize yourself as the man you long to be; see yourself in the exalted position you long to attain, a man of importance and power carrying weight in your community. No matter if you are only an errand boy or a clerk, see yourself as a partner in your concern, or a proprietor of a business of your own. There is nothing more potent in drawing your heart's desire to you than visualizing that desire, dreaming your dream, seeing yourself as the ideal man of your vision, filling the position in which your ambition would place you. Do this, and work with all your might for the attainment of your object on the physical plane, and nothing can hinder your success.

These are the means, consciously or unconsciously adopted, by which every successful man has ultimately attained his heart's desire.

Reading and thinking, visualizing and working along the lines of his ambition, the boy, Thomas Alva Edison, at the very first opportunity, when a newsboy on the Grand Trunk Railway, begins to actualize his desires by experimenting with chemicals in a baggage car which he had fitted up as a laboratory. He clings to his vision constantly, visualizes his dream of the magic possibilities of electricity; goes on discovering, experimenting, inventing, until we find him the world's greatest electrical inventor, the "Wizard of Menlo Park." His mind, working in harmony with Divine Mind, has wrought marvelous inventions out of the great cosmic intelligence, which is packed with potencies for those who can visualize with intensity and work with constancy.

What Edison has done, what all aspiring souls have done to make their dreams come true, you can do. Cling to your vision and work.

There is a power in man, back of the flesh, but not of it, working in harmony with the Divine Intelligence in the great cosmic ocean of energy, of limitless supply, that is, to-day, performing miracles in invention, in agriculture, in commerce, in industry. This power, which is creative and everywhere operative, is destined to lift every created thing up to the peak of its possibilities. It is latent in you, awaiting expression, awaiting your coöperation to realize your ambition. The first step toward utilizing it is to visualize the ideal of what you want to make real, the ideal of the man or the woman you aim to be, and the things you want to do. Without this initial step the further process of creating is impossible.

No matter what happens, always hold fast to the thought that you can be what you long to be; that you can do the thing you want to do, and picture yourself always as succeeding in what you desire to come true in your life. No matter how urgent duties or obligations may for a time hold you back, how circumstances and conditions may contradict the possibility of your success; how people, even your own people, may blame or misunderstand you, may even call you a crank, crazy, a conceited egotist, hold fast to your faith in your dream, in yourself. Cling to your vision, nurse it, for it is the God-inspired model by which He is urging you to shape your life.

CHAPTER X

WHAT DISCOURAGEMENT DOES TO YOU—HOW TO CURE IT

Discouragement has done more to dwarf the efforts of the race, has thwarted more careers, stunted and starved more lives, than any other one agent.

Never make a decision when downhearted. Never let the weak side of your nature take control.

You are not capable of correct judgment when fear or doubt or despondency is in your mind. Sound judgment comes from a perfectly normal brain.

Have you the grit and pluck to stand all sorts of discouragement and to struggle on after failure without losing heart; to get up again every time you fall? Can you stand criticism, misunderstanding, abuse, without flinching or weakening? Have you the perseverance to go on when others turn back, to continue the fight when everybody around you is giving up? If you can do this you are a winner. Nothing can hold you back from your goal.

"You can't do it!" keeps more people with splendid ability in mediocrity than almost any other thing. "You can't do it!" meets you everywhere in life. At every turn you propose to take, you will find some one to warn you away, to tell you not to take that road, that it will lead to disaster. Unless you have unusual pluck, an iron will and a determination which never wavers, you are likely to become discouraged, and when you are once discouraged your initiative is deadened and your power paralyzed.

SOMEONE says: "Discouragement hides God's means and methods." It does more.

It hides God himself; it blots out of sight about everything that is helpful and friendly to us. It paralyzes our ability, our courage, our self-confidence; it destroys our efficiency and cuts down the effectiveness of every one of our faculties.

Every physician knows how discouragement affects the cure of a patient,—delays it, and often makes it impossible. The sick man who is cheerful, hopeful of his restoration to health, has ten chances to one for recovery compared with the one who is blue and despondent. Discouragement breaks the spirit, and when a man's spirit is broken he has no heart for anything. He is beaten in life's battle. A broken spirit, the loss of hope and courage, causes more failures, more suicides, more insanity, than almost anything else. I wish it were possible to show victims of discouragement what it does to them—how it destroys their morale, and tears down what they have built up in their creative, hopeful moments.

Only a short time ago I read the story of a fine young man who became the victim of discouragement. After losing his position, during a period of business depression, this man would start out every morning to hunt for another; and every night he would come home disappointed, but, for a long time, not discouraged, always believing that he would ultimately get a job.

This had been going on for weeks, when one night he was late in returning, and his wife, watching at the window until it was too dark to see any more, drew down the shades and tried in busying herself with housewifely tasks to dispel the sudden feeling of anxiety that gripped her. When her husband came an hour later, she noticed that some depressing influence seemed to have been working upon him; that he was not quite as hopeful as he had been. She cheered him up as usual, gave him his supper, encouraged him in every possible way, and sent him to bed comforted. Next morning he tried to talk hopefully, and when he was ready to start for the city, assured her that he was going to do his best. But it was evident he didn't feel quite as sure of himself, quite as self-confident, as he had been.

Watching at the window for his return that evening, the faithful wife was surprised to see that he was not alone. A shadowy, sinister figure was at his side, talking very earnestly to him. It accompanied him to the gate and then suddenly vanished. The next evening the same sinister figure walked at his side, and the look of despair on the man's face frightened her. The third evening the wife waited and watched until long after dark, but no husband came. Numb with fear, she sat through the long night at the window, where she kept a light burning until daylight, but no husband, and no word from him, came to her.

As soon as life began to stir in the neighborhood she went out for a morning paper, and the first item that caught her eye was the suicide of a man who had thrown himself into the river and was drowned. Filled with foreboding, she rushed to the morgue where the newspaper stated the body had been taken, and there her fears were verified. The body of the drowned man was that of her husband.

The young man had toward the end become so discouraged by the hideous pictures his doubts and fears threw upon the screen of his mind that he became mentally unbalanced, and in despair ended his life. In those last days discouragement was so persistently at his side, telling him it was no use looking for a job, that he would never get one, that it was visualized by him as a reality, and actually became visible to the sensitive, sympathetic eyes of his wife.

Right now I know a number of people who are so depressed and demoralized by pessimistic, discouraged thinking, that they are seriously endangering their future success and the happiness of their whole lives. Because they are temporarily out of employment, discouragement has taken hold of them and filled their minds with such black, depressing pictures that they go about as do the insane in the beautiful grounds allotted to them. They see only the gloomy mental world their thoughts have constructed, and are unaware of the bright, cheerful, sunlit world all around them. They are, in fact, temporarily insane, because all mental depression, whatever the immediate cause, is in some degree mental derangement, the confusion and unhappiness which are always the results of wrong thinking.

It is well known that worry and discouragement cause chemical changes in the body which actually produce chemical poisons.

These poisons lower the resisting power of both body and mind and leave the sufferer a prey to all sorts of unfortunate results. There are multitudes of people to-day in poor health and in poor circumstances, plodding along in discontent and unhappiness, when they might be happy and doing superb things were they not the victims of discouraging conditions, conditions which are largely the result of their fear and worry. Their minds are out of joint, unhinged, and unfit for the work of to-day, because they are divided between looking forward to the future, anticipating all sorts of evils and misfortunes, and looking backward to the past, regretting whatever they had or had not done.

One of the saddest things in my work is the cry of unhappiness that comes to me from people who have lost their courage and ambition. They write me that they have ruined their careers, and that all they can do now is to live on in a very hopeless and unhappy way. "Oh, if I hadn't quit in a moment of discouragement!" they wail: "If I hadn't yielded to homesickness and left college!" "If I had only stuck to my trade, to my law practice, to my engineering work a little longer, until success came to me; if I had only kept on, how different things would be to-day! But I lost heart, got blue and discouraged and decided to try something easier. I have never been happy or satisfied with myself since I played the coward and turned back, but it is too late to make a change."

There are millions of people in inferior or mediocre positions to-day who might be doing big things had they not yielded to discouragement at the start and ruined the promise of their lives. Nine-tenths of the men and women in the great failure army are there because they were not prepared to meet obstacles, setbacks, and were frightened when they confronted them. They didn't have the vision that sees beyond obstacles and holds on in spite of unexpected difficulties, disappointments, and reverses.

Some people are always at home to the "blues." They are, as Carlyle says, "rich in the power to be miserable." I know a woman whose mind is so adjusted to despondency and discouragement that a very little thing brings on a fit of the "blues." She seems to be always ready to receive the whole blue family, and the first one that gets admission to her mind drags in his relatives,—discouragement, despondency, despair, fear, worry, and all the rest. They hold her in thrall for days together, driving out everything else, all happiness, courage, confidence, her very sanity.

Indulgence in the "blues," in morbid, despondent moods, is dangerous to character development and success. After a while it becomes a settled habit, a disease, and every little setback, every little disappointment, throws the sufferer off his balance, kills his enthusiasm and his zest for work, lowers his efficiency and, for the time being, his ability. In the end it acts like creeping paralysis and robs him of all initiative, all power and energy, all desire even to do. I am acquainted with a man whose habitual despondency has starved and stunted his whole life. He is a striking illustration of the destructive power of unhappy thoughts. He gives one the impression of great possibilities never expressed. His forces are shut up within him. He is always full of fear, worry, and anxiety. Discouragement envelops him like a mantle. His attitude, his manner, his expression, his speech, all indicate a shrink-ing and shriveling, an impotence which is due to his unfortunate moods. He is discontented, restless, unhappy, suffering from the sense of a thwarted ambition, and although he has worked very hard all his life his morbid men-tality and discouraged outlook have cut down his efficiency more than fifty per cent, and left him away behind where a man of his natural ability should be.

One of the marks of a strong soul, one who is anchored in faith, is the ability to conquer discouragement, melancholia, the "blues," all tendencies to cowardice and self-pity. No matter what happens, what obstacles or trials push such souls back, or for a time press them down, they never lose hope or give way under disappointments and failures. It is not that they do not feel those things, but that they will not suffer them to turn them aside from their purpose, to defeat their ambition.

Now the greatest obstacles to our success are in our minds, and there is no one so weak that he cannot overcome the most destructive enemy thoughts by the application of mental chemistry; that is, by calling to his aid the

antidotes for the enemy thoughts, and training his mind to face the light instead of
the darkness. A discouraging, despondent
thought can instantly be neutralized by a
courageous, hopeful thought, just as an acid
can instantly be neutralized by an alkali. The
mental law is as scientific as the physical. We
cannot hold two opposite thoughts in the mind
at the same time, one neutralizes or drives out
the other. We can always crowd out a negative, destructive fear thought, by persistently
holding in mind its opposite,—a positive,
courageous, constructive thought.

"Whistling to keep up courage is no mere
figure of speech," said William James, the
great psychologist. "On the other hand, sit
all day in a moping posture, sigh and reply to
everything in a dismal voice and your melancholy lingers." That is, by our thoughts and
acts we can draw to ourselves courage or discouragement. In other words, we can change
our mental attitude as we will; and to change
our thought is to change our condition.

For instance, if you are looking for a job
and don't find one; if you have had reverses,
and don't know where your next dollar is com-

ing from; if you are a round peg in a square hole; if you have made mistakes; if for any reason you are discouraged and tempted to retreat before the enemy, instead of going about with a defeated, gloomy, despondent air, turn about face at once and assume the attitude of a victor in life. Say to yourself: "God did not create any man to be a failure. He gave to all his children qualities that command success, each in his own field. All we need is to use them. I am success-organized, because I partake of the attributes of the Creator of the universe, the Omnipotent One. I will now use the divine power within me to do the thing I want to do; to get the position I desire; to satisfy all my needs. Failure cannot come near me. I am a success now, because I am one with All-Power."

Resolutely hold this mental attitude, and you will be surprised to find what courage it will give you, and how your difficulties will wilt before it.

General Foch says that a lost battle is a battle you think you can't win. Multitudes of battles have been won by the persistent determination of a single general who had not given up hope when all others had.

"*You* are beaten; this army is not beaten," has ever been the reply of great generals to the discouraged one who wanted to give up the battle as lost. It is the Joffres, the Fochs, the Grants, the men of indomitable faith and courage, who have ever wrung victory from defeat.

All down through history glorious victories have been won, not by masses of men, but by single individuals who had superb courage, a mighty faith in themselves and in their undertaking, an unflinching determination to succeed. In innumerable instances such brave souls had saved the day when their comrades had given up because they saw nothing but defeat, where the will to conquer had seen only victory.

There is somebody not far from you at this moment, my doubting, discouraged friend, who could step into your place and command victory with the resources which you think so inadequate for the work you have to do. There is somebody who has no more ability than you have who could see an unusual opportunity in the situation which you find so hopeless, so discouraging.

A great scientist said that when he encountered what seemed an unconquerable obstacle he invariably found himself upon the brink of some important discovery. The time above all others when it is most important for a man to hold fast to his faith and courage is when the way is so dark that he cannot see ahead. If you push on toward your goal when everything seems going against you, when doubt and discouragement are doing their best to make you give up, turn back, turn coward and quitter, then is the time when you are closer to victory than you dream of. If you never lose your conviction in your divine God-given power to win out in spite of handicaps or any obstacles that may arise in your path, nothing can defeat you, because you are in conscious partnership with Omnipotence.

WHAT AM I?

I am the great paralyzer of ability, the murderer of aspiration and ambition, the destroyer of energy, the killer of opportunity.

I am the cause of more suffering, more human misery and loss, more tragedies and wretchedness than any other one thing.

I have cursed more human beings, arrested the development of more fine ability, strangled more genius and stifled more talent than anything else in the world.

I have shortened vast multitudes of lives and sent more people to the insane asylum, to crime and suicide than men dream of.

I cause chemical changes in the brain which cripple efficiency and ruin careers.

I deprive human beings of more things that are good for them, things that fit their nature, and that they were intended to enjoy, than any other one agent.

I cause men and women to wear poor, shabby clothes, to look dejected and forlorn, when it is the right of every human being to look up, to be well-dressed, attractive, and happy.

I shut out the sun of hope and cause men to see everything in a distorted light because I make them look on the shadow side of things.

I devitalize people and make chronic invalids of men and women who should be enjoying perfect health.

I am the devil's most effective instrument.

If he can once get the bare suggestion of me into the human consciousness at the psychological moment, he can work destruction to the most ambitious, the greatest genius.

I starve and stunt minds, and keep vast multitudes of people in ignorance.

I usually attack a man when he is down, when things have gone wrong, and he is feeling blue. When he is tired, fatigued, devitalized, I find an easy entrance to his mind, because then his courage is not so keen, his brain is not so alert, and he has less dare in his nature.

I find that the best time to work on my victims is in the afternoon. In the morning men are too vigorous mentally, have too much vitality and energy, too much courage, to give in to me, but along in the afternoon when the body and brain begin to weary of work, and the whole man feels a bit fagged, I can tackle the great mental scheme which was in the forefront of the brain in the forenoon, when the faculties were clean-cut, and unless my victim is alert I soon have him under my control.

I am the greatest human deceiver. Once I get into the mind, I can make a giant believe he is a pygmy, and of no account. I can cut down his self-respect until in his own estimation he is a very ordinary man.

I have a twin brother, Doubt, who is called the great traitor. He is always ready to help me to finish my little game. We work together, and when under our control it is impossible for a man to be resourceful, original, or effective.

I creep into a man's mind after he has resolved to branch out on new lines, to step out from the beaten path and blaze his own way, and weaken his ardor, dampen his enthusiasm, and make him feel inefficient and helpless. I whisper in his ear, "Go slow; better be careful. Many abler men than you have fallen down trying to do that very thing. It is not the time to start this thing; you had better wait, wait, wait."

I haven't a single redeeming thing in my nature, and yet I have more influence with the human race than has any one of the finer, nobler qualities which help to bring man up to the height of his possibilities.

I AM DISCOURAGEMENT

CHAPTER XI

HOW TO MAKE YOUR SUBCONSCIOUS MIND
WORK FOR YOU

When all men know how to make the subconscious work for them there will be no poor people, none in distress or suffering, in pain or ill health; no one will be unhappy, no one will be a victim of thwarted ambitions.

Your subconscious mind is like a garden, and you must be very careful what you plant there. Every thought, every emotion, every suggestion is a seed planted in the subconscious soil, and will bring you a harvest like itself. It doesn't matter what kind of thought seeds you plant, whether poverty or prosperity, failure or success, happiness or misery, you will reap a harvest in kind.

If you impress vividly, intensely, and persistently, upon the creative mind in the great within of you, your determination to be what you long to be; if you register your vow to succeed in doing what you long to do; and do your level best to actualize your longings, nothing in the world can stand in the way of your success.

Every great inventor, every great discoverer, every great genius has felt the thrill of the divine inward force, that mysterious power back of the flesh but not of it, which has come to his aid in working out the device, the discovery, the book, the painting, the great musical composition, the poem, whatever he was trying to create or discover.

I PREDICT that within the next twenty-five years the average man, through his knowledge of the infinite power and possibilities of the subconscious mind, that mysterious force in the great within, will be able to accomplish more than the greatest minds of all time have ever dreamed of doing.

Science has revealed the mechanism of the body and mastered the secrets of its marvelous construction and action; but the mystery of mind is as yet but dimly understood. Very few have even a faint realization of its immense hidden powers.

The body becomes unconscious in sleep and all its voluntary activities cease. But the mind —what does it do when the body sleeps? We know it does not sleep, for when the body is wrapped in slumber the memory and imagination slip out of their house and go where they will. They wander in scenes of the past or they project themselves into the future. Now they are visiting in California, now in London, now in Paris, now they are among the stars. What embodiment do they assume? Or do they take visible form? They certainly seem to be completely independent of the body during sleep.

The new psychology explains the mystery of mind in a very simple way. It claims that

that part of the mind which continues active when we sleep is that marvelous force in the great within of us which, understood and rightly used, will enable man .to reach the heights of his limitless possibilities.

We know that we are tapping a new source of power. When we can do this intelligently, scientifically, we shall all be performing what hitherto have been regarded as miracles. We are just beginning to realize that the subconscious mind is the channel by which we connect with infinite supply; with the great creative processes of the universe; that through it man can tap the Infinite Mind and accomplish things that will dwarf to insignificance achievements that now excite our wonder and admiration.

Everything, so far as results are concerned, depends upon the degree of intelligence and conscious purpose with which we use the subconscious mind, for it is forever occupied registering on the invisible creative substance our every thought, emotion, desire, wish, or feeling. It never sleeps, but is incessantly working on the suggestions it receives from the conscious or objective mind. Your habitual thought, your convictions, your visions, your dreams, your beliefs, are all impressed upon it, and will ultimately be expressed in your life. In other words, your subconscious mind is your servant, and proceeds instantly, without quibbling, without questioning, no matter whether it is a big thing or a little thing, whether it is right or wrong, to obey the order, to follow the suggestion, you give it.

For instance, when you want to take an early train, or to get up in the middle of the night for some purpose, when you haven't been accustomed to do so, and you say to yourself, or hold the thought in mind before dropping to sleep, "I must wake up in time to get that train in the morning," or, "I must get up at one o'clock to-night," you are sure to awaken at almost the exact time you register, when, perhaps, you haven't been awake at that hour before in a year. You have no alarm clock; no one calls you; what wakes you up at just the right time? You probably never asked yourself the question, or thought about it. But it was that little faithful subconscious servant who was on the watch for you while you slept.

A similar thing is true of our appointments;

making dates or engagements for some time in the future. You agree to meet a man to-morrow or some day next week at a certain place and hour. You don't make any written record of it and the thing passes out of your mind. But when the time comes round you are reminded of your engagement. From long experience I know that that something inside of me will bring every engagement I make to my consciousness in time for me to attend to it. I don't keep thinking of it all the time. Not at all. I file it away in the within of me as I would file a business letter in my office for future reference. Then I dismiss it from my thought, knowing that it will be taken care of at the proper time.

The trained man learns to commit all sorts of things to his subconscious secretary, knowing from experience that it will serve him faithfully, not only in comparatively small things, such as awakening him at any desired hour in the night or early morning, constantly reminding him of his engagements, but also in the big serious problems of life. Edison says that when he is right up against a great problem in his work and has no idea in the world how to solve it, he simply sleeps over it, and many a time he wakes up in the morning to find his problem solved; it has been worked out for him while he slept in ways which he never dreamed of. The details of various inventions have been completed for him in this way.

I know a great many business and professional men who do as Mr. Edison does when serious problems confront them; they sleep on them before they make any decision. In fact, it is the commonest thing in the world, when we are considering some serious problem, for all of us to say: "I must sleep over that matter before deciding; it is so important." What does sleeping over such a matter mean? We may not understand or be able to explain, but what it really means is this: Your subconscious mind takes up the problem at the point where your conscious mind left it when you went to sleep, and in the morning you will find that it has been thought out for you. Your subconscious wisdom has entered into the transaction, given you the benefit of its advice and enabled you to make the right decision.

When all men know how to make the subconscious work for them there will be no poor people, none in distress or suffering, in pain or ill health; no one will be unhappy, a victim of thwarted ambitions. We shall know then that all we have to do to make our dreams come true, to be prosperous and happy, is to give our invisible secretary the right instructions and follow this up with the necessary effort.

Establishing in your subconscious mind the things that you want to come true, that you are ambitious to attain; impressing upon it the ideal of the man or woman you long to be, is the first step toward achievement. Hold the conviction in your consciousness that your own is already headed your way, work for it confidently in the realization that you can draw from the creative energy of the universal mind anything you desire, and it will surely come to you, because you will thus start the process of creation in the great within of you.

Consciously or unconsciously put in motion, these are the initial steps that have led to the production of every great work of art and genius in the world. They were adopted in the production of our railroads, our ships, our homes, our great monuments and buildings, our cities, our telegraph, telephone, and wireless systems, our airplanes, and all the marvels of modern inventions. Edison says he is only a medium for transmitting from the great cosmic intelligence and energy which fill the universe a few of the infinite number of devices which are destined to emancipate human beings from every form of drudgery. He believes that the best things he has given to the world have been merely passed along through him to his fellow men from the Infinite Source of all supply.

While the subconscious mind is all-powerful in working out the pattern or idea we give it, of itself it does not originate, so it will make all the difference in the world to you what sort of material you give your subconscious mind to work on. You can make it an enemy or a friend, for it will do the thing which injures you just as quickly as the thing which blesses you. Not through malice, but because it has no discriminating power any more than the soil in which the farmer sows his seed.

If the farmer should make a mistake and sow thistle seed instead of wheat, the soil doesn't say to him, "My friend, you have made a mistake. You have been sowing thistle seed instead of wheat, so we will change the law, that you may get what you thought you were going to get." No, the soil will always give us a harvest like our sowing. If we sow thistle seed it will be just as faithful in producing thistles as it will in producing wheat or cabbages or potatoes. We sow the seed and nature gives us a corresponding harvest; that is the law on the physical plane. It is exactly the same on the mental plane. The subconscious mind is like the soil, passive. The objective mind uses it, gives its commands or suggestions, which it carries out according to their nature. That is, the objective or conscious mind sows the seed in word, motive, thought or act, and the subconscious mind gives us back our own; always the thing that corresponds to what we impressed on it.

In other words, the subconscious mind has no choice but to follow the lead we give it. Hence, how important it is that our instructions to this invisible servant should be for our good and not for our harm; that we should saturate it, not with the things we do not want, the things we hate and fear and worry about, but the things we long for and are striving to attain.

If you are working hard, and yet not progressing toward your ideal; if you are in poverty and wretchedness, though constantly struggling to get away from those conditions; you are not obeying the law which governs the subconscious. Your thought is at fault; you are thinking poverty, thinking failure; your mind is filled with doubts and fears; you are working against the law instead of with it; you are neutralizing all your efforts by your wrong mental attitude.

Some people by their indomitable faith and self-confidence get hold of the dormant powers of the great within of themselves and unconsciously work with the law which governs them. Wherever a man or a woman is doing unusual things, struggling heroically to accomplish some great purpose, you find one who consciously or unconsciously is obeying this law, by making tremendous demands upon the subconscious; by registering his life purposes with such tremendous intensity and working so persistently, so confidently, along that line that his purpose is unfailingly carried

out.   Luther Burbank, for example, has done
and is doing tremendous things in the plant
world because he makes tremendous demands
upon the mighty agent within, his subconscious mind or self.   He does not neutralize
the demands by doubts and fears as to whether
they will be carried out or not.   He makes his
demands, gives his orders, persistently, em-
phatically, with vigor and determination, and
they are faithfully executed.   By the same
means, consciously or unconsciously used,
Madam Curie has made some of the most remarkable discoveries in the scientific world.
We can all accomplish our ends, attain our
life ambition by doing as they and all other
great achievers are doing—working with law.

We are not, as we were taught to believe in
the past, so many separate little bits of mind
thrown off into space to struggle for ourselves;
we are all a part of the infinite mind, the cosmic intelligence and energy of the universe.
We are the creation of the one Supreme Mind
which called all things out of the unseen, and
since the created must partake of the qualities
of the Creator, man must partake of the qualities of omniscience, of omnipotence, of the Su-

preme Mind that gave man dominion over the earth and everything on it. This means that we are really, so far as this earth is concerned, in partnership with God, that we are co-creators with the great creative intelligence which is everywhere active in the universe.

The marvelous accomplishments of man within the past few centuries can only be accounted for through his coöperation with his Creator. It is the spirit of God in man working in harmony with the spirit of God in the great cosmic intelligence of the universe which has made possible within the past half century achievements in science, in invention, in discovery that our ancestors would have ridiculed —if any one dared to suggest them as possibilities—as the imaginings of the insane. Wireless telegraphy and telephony, the automobile, the airplane; the harnessing of electricity to do the work in our factories, in our homes; the reconstruction of the body by great surgeons, the discoveries in astronomy; cables under oceans, connecting the ends of the earth; the construction of railroads under rivers and under the streets of our teeming cities; the works of scientific men in every field, of the great agriculturists, horticulturists and naturalists, and the great animal breeders who are doing in the animal world what the Burbanks are doing in the plant world—all these things are the results of man's reaching out into the great creative energy and in coöperation with Omnipotence molding it to his purposes.

The dictum of science is that "Nature unaided fails." In other words, man is God's working partner on this earth, his work being to lift everything upon it, including man himself, to the highest possibility of the divine plan. There is a power in man back of the flesh, which, working with the divine cosmic intelligence, will enable him to do things that at present we can hardly conceive of. Nothing we can imagine or dream of will be impossible of achievement, because we are a real part of the creative power which performs miracles throughout the universe. That is, apparent miracles, for everything follows a law which is never violated in order to perform what seem to us miracles.

In the consciousness of the mighty possibilities of the subconscious mind to tap the great universal mind lies the secret of infinite creative principle, of limitless power. There are powers in your subconscious mind which, if aroused and utilized, would help you do what others tell you is "impossible." Your ideal, your heart's desire, however unattainable it may seem at present, is a prophecy of what will come true in your life if you do your part.

It is only in our extremities that we touch our real power, that we unconsciously have recourse to the great within. There are multitudes of people in the failure army to-day, with scarcely energy enough to keep them alive, who have forces slumbering deep within themselves which, if they could only be awakened, would enable them to do wonderful things.

The great trouble with most of us, even those who have studied along this line, is that our demands upon ourselves are so feeble, the call upon the great within of us is so weak and so intermittent, that it makes no vital or permanent impression upon the creative energies; it lacks the force and persistency that transmute desires into realities. When we realize that it is through our subconscious selves, in the great within of us, that we make wireless connection with the All-Supply, with all possible joy and satisfaction; that it is here the great creative processes which make our dreams come true are started, it seems strange that we don't use this great force to better advantage.

When the necessary conditions are fulfilled the law that governs the subconscious operates unerringly. Work with the law instead of against it and nothing can hinder your success. In other words, let your subconscious mind help instead of hinder you. Give it the right thought, the right instruction, the right ideals to work on; give it success thoughts instead of failure thoughts, bright cheerful, hopeful thoughts instead of gloomy discouraging ones; never hold a thought that does not correspond with your ideal or ambition; no matter what conditions are, what obstacles stand in your way, persist in vividly visualizing your success, never letting a doubt or fear thought come between you and the confident belief that you will get the thing you long for and are working for with all your heart, and you will be amazed at what your faithful secretary, working in harmony with creative intelligence, will do for you.

The interior creative forces are more active during the night than in the day time, and are especially susceptible to the suggestions they receive before we fall asleep. During sleep the conscious mind is not active, and consequently the subconscious mind operates uninterruptedly, without any of the objections or hindrances which it is constantly bringing up during the day. Therefore it is of the greatest importance that you give the subconscious the right message, the right model on which to work during the night.

Do this before you drop to sleep and it will work for the attainment of your ambition, your desire, all night. Never allow yourself to fall asleep in a doubting, despondent mood. Do not hinder the operation of the creative intelligence at any time by doubt, or fear. Doubt is the great enemy which has neutralized the efforts, and killed the success of multitudes of people. Live always in the consciousness that you are a success in whatever you are trying to do and the creative processes within you, faithfully working according to the model you give them, will produce whatever you desire.

CHAPTER XII

THINKING HEALTH AND PROSPERITY INTO THE CELLS OF YOUR BODY

Every cell in us thinks.—THOMAS A. EDISON.

Each cell in the body is a conscious intelligent being.
PROFESSOR NELS QUEVLI.

Think and say regarding yourself and your future only that which you wish to come true.

As every cell in your body is constantly being made new, why not put new thoughts, new life, into your cells and not drag along with you all the old skeletons of the past?

The cell minds all through your body know whether you are master or not. They know whether you go through the world as conqueror or conquered, as a master or a slave, and they act accordingly. They fling back into your life the reflection of your thoughts, your motives, your convictions. Your condition will correspond with the mental attitude they reflect.

Thinking wholeness, completeness, perfection, into the cells will encourage and stimulate them. The functioning of all the cells of the body, of the various organs, is lowered when we are thinking black, discouraging thoughts, and all of our mental faculties correspond with our physical condition.

WHEN physicians told Jane Addams, a young girl just graduated from college, that she could not live more than six months, she said, *"All right, I will take that six months to*

144

get as near as I can to the one thing I want to do for humanity."

What happened? The firm expression of her determination to do the thing that lay nearest to her heart registered itself so indelibly on the cells in every remotest part of her body, from her brain center to the tips of her fingers, and downward to the points of her toes, that they began immediately to build for health. Eight years after the medical authority of that time had given her six months to live, she started Hull House, the world-famous Chicago settlement. To-day she is an international figure, a leader in different phases of the great modern movement for world betterment.

If instead of giving them her positive ringing message for life and work, Jane Addams had impressed upon the cells of her body the negative pronouncement of her physicians, and told them that she was going to die in six months, what would have happened? She would have died; for the cells would have accepted one suggestion as readily as the other. Instead of setting to work to repair and upbuild the body, they would have quit work;

the various organs and tissues would have dis-integrated, and the world would never have heard of Jane Addams or her great work.

When we get a thorough understanding of the power that Miss Addams unconsciously used when she cast the thought of death out of her mind and replaced it with the life thought, we can build into the very structure of our bodies whatever we wish them to express. If we are dissatisfied with the bodies we now have, we can literally build new ones, for every one of the billions of tiny cells that compose the human body is a living, thinking, working en-tity, which, like the sensitive plate of a camera, records in its structure the image of every emo-tion, thought, impression, or passion that passes through our consciousness.

The author of that marvelously interesting book, "Cell Intelligence" says: "The cell is a conscious intelligent being, and by reason thereof plans and builds all plants and animals in the same manner as man constructs houses, railroads, and other structures." That is, every cell does its part in building the body, setting the life along the lines we suggest, just as the mason, the bricklayer, the carpenter, and other workers construct a house in accordance with the lines of the architect's plan. Not only that, but scientists now believe that the cells which constitute the various organs of the body,—the brain, the heart, the liver, the kidneys, the lungs, etc.,—have what is called "organ intelligence," and that these cells are susceptible to mental suggestion for the health or disease of their particular organ. In other words, the little community of cells that form the heart think and work for the heart; the brain community work for the brain; the stomach community, for the stomach, and so on; and all together make a huge army of little body workers, responding instantly to whatever thought we impress on them.

If, for instance, there should be a disease tendency lurking in any part of your body; if your digestive organs, your heart, your kidneys, your liver, or some other organ, should not be functioning normally, by sending encouraging, energizing, uplifting thoughts, the suggestion of health and wholeness, to the community cells, and by living rightly, you can neutralize the disease tendency and bring the organ back to normalcy. The intelligent cells

will do exactly as your thought suggests—
work for health and the elimination of the disease tendency. On precisely the same principle, the opposite thought,—the thought of
disease, of abnormalcy,—suggested to these
little cell minds, which are already tending to
disease, to abnormalcy, will aggravate the
trouble and hasten the development of the
lurking disease in the system.

I have heard a man curse his stomach and his
digestive organs for not digesting his food
properly. Every time he sits down to the table
he begins to complain about the food hurting
him: "I can't eat this," he will say. "My
stomach can't take care of it. I can't digest
this; I can't digest that. It is bound to come
back on me if I attempt to eat it. I wish I
had a decent stomach instead of the good-for-
nothing thing I have." Now, how can any intelligent man expect the coöperation of his
stomach and his digestive organs when he is
sending such discordant thoughts into their
cell minds? When he is constantly blaming
and cursing those organs for not functioning
normally, upbraiding them for giving him pain
and distress, how can he expect them to do

their best work and serve him cheerfully and efficiently? Those organs are like children or employees, and a man might just as reasonably expect to get cheerful, willing, efficient service from his children or his employees by cursing, scolding, and abusing them as to get it from his bodily organs when he does this.

The state of your body is a reflection of your habitual thought about it, your general mental attitude and beliefs regarding your various organs. When you think of your heart as weak, of your liver as sluggish, of your kidneys as diseased; when you say, "I'm sick; I'm discouraged; I'm tired; I'm down and out; I'm all in; all used up; I don't feel like anything," do you know what you are doing to the little cell minds all through your body? You are weakening and demoralizing them; you are stamping your discouraged, despondent thought, the picture of weakness, of inefficiency, on their very structure, and their functioning will be accordingly deteriorated. The weak, discouraged, pessimistic, sick or diseased thought produces a condition like itself in every cell in the body, and the body suffers in proportion to the persistence of such thoughts. They tend to tear down, to destroy the body tissues, to paralyze the life functions.

The real basis of all forms of mental healing is the fact that the cells of the body are all alive and intelligent; that they respond to our thought, to our intelligence, to our suggestions to them. It makes a great difference to the mental healer to know that instead of sending his thought into a mass of dead cells, every one is not only alive, but is just as responsive to his mental attitude as an intelligent child would be. He knows that his health thought, his uplift thought, the thought of their wholeness and completeness, the suggestion of their divine origin, of their power to upbuild the body, to renew its strength and vigor, sends a thrill of encouragement, of hope and assurance through every one of them, and starts them on their task of neutralizing the disease thought and renewing the health and vitality of his patient.

Be careful what you think into these little cell minds of your body, my friend, for it will come back to you not only in your physical condition but in every aspect of your life. For example, when you think bad luck into them, when you are thinking how unlucky you are, telling everybody about it, saying that fate is against you, and that no matter what you do you can't get ahead, you are discouraging these little cell minds, just as you do when you think disease and ill health into them. You paralyze them, in other words, and instead of functioning normally, they function abnormally, and your health, your chances of success, your mentality, your power to overcome the obstacles in your way, are all seriously affected. There is a letting down all along the line. Your discouraged, pessimistic thoughts have robbed you of energy and pep; demagnetized you for the very things you are trying to attract,—health and prosperity.

The problem of maintaining physical vigor, abounding health, the magnetic energy that draws things to us out of the cosmic intelligence, is solved when you learn how to keep all of the little cell minds which form the different tissues of the body organs in perfect condition, so that they will be alert, happy, cheerful, hopeful. They will then reflect the maximum of your creative thought, the maximum of vigor and robustness, of physical and mental power, for it is in these little building, creative centers that our grit and our determination are nourished. Here is where we get our energy, our motive power, and hence we must be very careful what we whisper into these little cell minds, whether encouragement or discouragement, hope or despair, health or disease, poverty or prosperity. They are, so to speak, the tiny children of the larger mind and are very susceptible to what the larger mind thinks, the instructions it sends them, the various impulses which go out from the central station of the body—the brain.

If a sick, weak man wants to be strong and well, he must impress a strong, healthy picture of himself on the cells that are trying to repair, to rebuild him. He must hold the image of himself as he would like to be, not as he is. Instead of this many sick people think or say to themselves something like this: "Oh, how sick I am. I feel so weak that I'm afraid I never shall be well again. I shall never be able to do anything in the world. My ambition only mocks and tortures me, because I shall never be able to realize it. Looks as if my work here was done. This disease has gotten such a hold upon me that it will never let go. Why is it that the Creator allows human beings to suffer this way, tortures them with the ambition to do something which they can never do, never have the strength to do?"

How little people realize that when they hold such thoughts, visualize themselves in a weak, despairing, dying condition, they are just as surely committing suicide as if they were to take a slow poison. Every cell in the body is poisoned and made helpless by the wrong thought.

If you picture the billions of cells in your body as tiny individualities, little dancers, who are dancing to whatever tune you give them, you will get some idea of the action of your mind upon them in uplifting or depressing you; for they dance the life dance or the death dance, the sick dance or the health dance, the poverty dance or the prosperity dance, the love dance or the hate dance, the happiness dance or the misery dance, the success dance or the failure dance, in response to whatever thought tune you give them.

Many people make themselves invalids or semi-invalids all their lives by their down-

dragging thought tunes, holding the discouraged conviction that they never will be well,
that they are always going to be more or less
helpless. If they changed their conviction
their physical condition would immediately
change. This has been proved true time and
time again by the apparent miracles wrought
by mental healers, who simply changed the
trend of the patient's mind, turned his thought
from abnormal, diseased conditions to healthful, wholesome conditions. Then the little cells
began to dance to the new tune, the tune of
life, of wholeness, and the body at once re-
sponded in renewed vitality and vigor.

Nothing will do more toward making your
life, your personality, your environment what
you want them to be than the daily habit of
thinking into the cell minds of your body what
you wish them to express,—health, prosperity,
success, happiness, joy, good-will, harmony,
peace, divine power and energy. You can do
this every morning before you start out to your
daily task and every little while during the day
when you have a bit of leisure.

The important thing is to keep out of the
mind all enemy thoughts. The moment any

of these gain entrance, and are permitted to remain, they begin to tear down and destroy. They play havoc with your efficiency, with your health and happiness. If anything occurs during the day to disturb your poise or your self-control, if you feel angry impulses rising within you, recollect yourself as quickly as possible and get control again, for nothing is more hurtful to the whole man or woman than mental inharmony of any nature. You can speak peace into the billions of turbulent cells, just as Christ spoke peace to the turbulent waters of the sea. When you give them the harmony keynote they will respond. They will always reflect what you suggest to them. When the master mind speaks they obey. Change your inharmonious thought and you change the condition of the billions of little cell entities in your body. In short, whatever you want your life to express, think it into those entities and it will come to pass; for they are your partners, doing team work with you.

Think of every cell in your body as a little worker for you, a little producer, a little intelligent separate entity, coöperating with the one great universal intelligence, the great cosmic purpose. Picture the cells collectively as a myriad army welded together by Supreme Power and working together to make you a dominant, forceful personality, a man or a woman capable of conquering any environment, mastering any unfortunate conditions that wrong thinking may have brought into manifestation. Never allow yourself to think weakness, poverty or poverty-stricken conditions into them or want or limitation of any kind. You are God's child; think accordingly. Think in keeping with your immortal inheritance. Think big, because you are big. Think generously, because you are made to express generosity, not picayuneness. You are not made for cheeseparing economy, but for largeness of living; you were made for the life abundant, not for the pinched, stunted, starved life.

The possibilities of the life which keys the cell minds to the right thought is beyond all calculation. Every thought of power, every thought of health, every thought of love, every truth thought, every beauty thought, every thought of perfection, of wholeness, of vigor of mind and body, every thought of God will attune your mind and body to the power and perfection of the creative plan of Divine Mind.

Thinking health, thinking happiness, thinking truth, thinking power and perfection, prosperity, success, into the little cell minds of the body will, in the future, be a very important part of every child's training. Their lives from the start will be keyed right; the little cell workers will get the right command, the right mental picture, and they will build for health, prosperity, and success, not for weakness, poverty, and failure.

Right thinking, making the cells work in the right way, of construction instead of destruction, will banish from the earth two of the greatest handicaps of the race—disease and poverty.

WHAT AM I?

I am the vital principle of life—the greatest of all success and happiness assets.

I am that which gives the plus quality to human beings. I put pep, ginger, vim, into human effort.

I am the source of physical and mental power. I give the body vigor and buoyancy, the brain vital energy and originality.

I am your best friend—the friend of the high and lowly, the rich and the poor alike—but, be he king or beggar, who violates my laws must pay the penalty.

I am often sought in vain by the man who rides in his limousine, but am generally found in the company of the man who walks to his work and takes plenty of exercise.

I am the great multiplier of ability, the buttress of initiative, of courage, of self-confidence, the backbone of enthusiasm, without which nothing worth while was ever accomplished.

I am the greatest constructive power in the life of man. Without me his faith weakens, his ambition sags, his ardor oozes out, his courage faints, his self-confidence departs, his accomplishment is *nil*.

Without me wealth is a mockery, a palatial home a bitter disappointment.

Next to life itself, I am the greatest gift God has given to man; the millionaire who has lost me in piling up his fortune would give all his millions to get me back again.

I am that which gives buoyancy to life, which makes you magnetic, joyous, forceful, which brings out your resourcefulness and inventiveness, that which raises efficiency to its maximum and enables you to make the most of your ability.

I increase every one of your forty or fifty mental faculties a hundredfold. I am the leader of them all. When I am present they are up, at their best; when I am absent, they are down, at their worst.

I am the friend of progress, the stimulator of ambition, the encourager of effort, the great essential to efficiency, to success, the promoter of long life and happiness.

I am a joy bringer. Where I go, good cheer goes. Where I am not, depression, discouragement, the "blues," are present. My absence means declining powers, often thwarted ambition, blighted hopes, mediocrity, failure, a shortened life.

The wise man guards me as the apple of his eye; the fool often abuses and loses me through ignorance, indifference or neglect.

I AM GOOD HEALTH

CHAPTER XIII

HOW TO MAKE YOURSELF LUCKY

Believe with all your heart that you can and will do what you were made to do.

The "lucky" man never waits for something to turn up.

"Luck is the ability to recognize an opportunity and take advantage of it."

To make yourself lucky, choose the vocation nature fitted you for and then fling your life into it. Be all there.

Self-confidence and industry are the friends of good luck.

Good luck follows good sense, good judgment, good health, a gritty determination, a lofty ambition, and downright hard work. It follows the man who cultivates tact, courtesy, courage, self-confidence, will power, optimism, health, and good-will to all men.

A New York broker not long ago committed suicide because he thought luck, which had been a dominant factor in his life creed, had forsaken him. He had such faith in the fetish, luck, that, when he met with a series of Wall Street losses, he believed there was no further use in struggling against his destiny. Luck had turned its back on him, he declared, and

160

he had nothing more to live for. His dying words to his wife were, "Good luck to you."

Many a man, though he may not go so far as this Wall Street broker did, limits himself by a superstitious belief in good or ill luck. He is convinced that there is some fate or destiny, something beyond his control which determines the extent of his achievement, and that if this mysterious power fights against him, he will fail; if it helps him, he will succeed.

Nothing is so fatal to achievement as the belief in a blind destiny, in the fallacy that an effect can be brought about without a sufficient cause. Yet how many able-bodied people are waiting around for luck to solve their problems, waiting to get a lift from that mysterious, indefinable something which helps one man on and keeps another back, regardless of his own efforts. One might as well wait for luck to solve mathematical problems as to wait for it to solve any of his own life problems.

Man is master of his own destiny. The power to solve his problems is right inside of him. He makes the fate which downs him or lifts him up. Life is not a game of chance.

The Creator did not put us here to be the sport of circumstances, puppets to be tossed about by a cruel fate, which we could not control. He has given man a free will, an unfettered mind, and—

"Man makes his fate according to his mind;
            The weak, low spirit
Fortune makes her slave,
But she's a drudge when hectored by the brave.
            If Fate weave common thread
I'll change the doom
And with new purple weave a nobler loom."

"Why art thou cast down, oh, my soul!" There is that within you, my good friend, which is a great deal more than a match for anything that can try to down you. You have inherited a power from your Divine Parent which infinitely more than matches any defect or deficiency you may think you have inherited from your earthly parents, or any handicap in your environment. There is something of omnipotence in you, for you are the child of Omnipotence, and you must have inherited the qualities of your Creator.

No matter what happens to you, remember there is something in you bigger than any fate, something that can laugh at any cruel destiny, for you are your own fate, your own destiny.

There is a God in you, my friend. Assert your divinity. All you have to do is to tap the Eternal Mind, the great cosmic energy, and all power is yours. You are at the very source of the All-Supply.

"Luck is the ability to recognize an opportunity and take advantage of it," says Beatrice Fairfax, and if we accept her definition we must admit that there is such a thing as luck.

Perhaps you have heard of the young man who happened to be the only physician present in a crowd which gathered around a king's carriage when he was stricken with a fit in a street in London. The young doctor pressed through the crowd and said he could relieve the king by blood letting. The king revived and this incident was a great stepping-stone to the marvelous career of Ambrose Paré.

It sometimes happens that in a railroad wreck or some other great catastrophe an unknown man leaps into notoriety by some simple act which thousands of others could have performed as well. But the ability to seize the opportunity, and do the needed thing promptly and accurately, is due to the cultivation of one's initiative, the daily development of promptness and precision in caring for business affairs.

What you, my friend, may right now be calling your hard luck, may be the result of some weakness, some bad habit, which is thwarting your efforts, keeping from you the prosperity you desire. You may have peculiarities, objectionable traits, which are bars to your progress, stumbling-blocks in your path. Your bad luck may be lack of preparation, a poor education, insufficient training for your special work. Your foundation may be too small for any sort of a respectable life structure. Or, your bad luck may be indolence, a love of ease and pleasure, a desire to have a good time first of all, no matter what happens.

Good luck is the very opposite of all this. Every successful man knows that good luck follows the strong will, the earnest, persistent endeavor, good hard work, thorough preparation, the ambition to excel and a dead-in-earnest purpose.

The "lucky" man is the man who has been a closer thinker, a harder worker, than his "unlucky" neighbor. He is more practical, his life has been ruled by system and order.

Luck is like opportunity, it comes to those who work for it and are ready for it. Make the best possible use of your time, this will make you lucky.

If you are handicapped by the lack of an education you can get a fair equivalent of a college education, no matter how busy your life may be. Read and study during your spare moments. A multitude of men and women are educating themselves in this way every day, and are climbing up in the world in spite of a thousand obstacles and handicaps which you have never known.

If we should examine the careers of most men who are called "lucky," we should find that their success has its roots way back in their early youth, and that it has drawn its nourishment from many a battle in the struggle for supremacy over poverty and opposition. We should find that the "lucky" man is not a believer in luck, but in himself; that he has never waited for things "to turn up," or for luck to come his way. He has gone to work and turned things up, made luck come his way.

My experience has been that the men who are made of winning material do not talk of hard luck or cruel fate; they do not talk of being kept back by others. If a man has yeast in him he will rise; nothing can keep him back. Clear grit will attract more good luck than almost any other one thing I know of.

It is usually the lazy, the indolent, the pleasure-loving good-for-nothings, the weaklings, who are the firmest believers in luck. The mere fact that a man is always talking about his "hard luck," blaming his non-success, his defeats on someone else, or on unfortunate circumstances, is an admission that he is a weak man. It shows that he has not developed independence or strength of will, the mental fiber which overcomes obstacles.

There is everything in forming this habit of thinking of yourself as lucky, fortunate, of always seeing yourself as you would like to be, not as one who is inefficient and always blundering. Talk about yourself and of things as you wish they were, otherwise you will drive away what you long for and attract things which you wish to get rid of.

A business man whom I have known for some years has formed what might be called "the hard luck habit." If he invests in anything, he will say: "Of course, I'm sure to lose. It is just my luck. When I buy the market always begins to fall. The good things fly away when I purchase." He always thinks he is going to get the worst of it in whatever he undertakes. If he starts something new in his business, he immediately begins to talk gloomily about it. "It won't go, I have a feeling that it won't win out," he declares. He is always talking "hard luck," predicting that things are going to the bad, and that "it will have to be worse before it is better." This man hasn't nearly as much money as he had several years ago, and his losses have come largely from his sour mental outlook, his lack of confidence in his judgment, his perpetual anticipation of loss and evil, and his belief in an unkind fate.

There are multitudes of hard-working people who are continually driving away from them the very thing they are trying to get, because they do not hold the right attitude of mind. They lack the enthusiastic man's optimism, his faith and self-confidence,—all friends of good luck.

If you persist in looking and acting like a

failure, or a very mediocre or doubtful success; if you keep telling everybody how unlucky you are, and that you do not believe you will win out, because success is only for a favored few, those who have a pull, someone to boost them, you will be as much of a success as the actor who attempts to impersonate a certain character while looking, thinking, and acting exactly like the opposite.

Our thoughts and words are real forces which build or tear down. Who sees only failure is never a winner. It is the man who never sees anything but victory, who never acknowledges the possibility of defeat, that wins out. The man who tries to excuse his failure on the ground that he was doomed from the start by the bad cards fate dealt him, that he had to play the game with them, and that no amount of effort on his part could have materially altered the results, deceives himself.

I know a man who, whenever he misses a train, says, "I knew I wouldn't catch it! It was just my luck to miss it! I must have been born late." If he makes a blunder or an unfortunate mistake he will say, "I am unlucky about everything. I might have known it would turn out bad. If I bought gold dollars to-day they wouldn't be worth more than fifty cents to-morrow."

Now, my friend, talking disparagingly about yourself, depreciating yourself, is self-deterioration. The constant suggestion of your inferiority, of your defects or weaknesses, will interfere with your success in anything. You can't be lucky, you can't be successful, if you are all the time talking against yourself, for this will undermine your confidence in yourself and in your efficiency.

Hold a good opinion of yourself. Think highly of yourself. Learn to appreciate your ability and to respect yourself, not egotistically or from a selfish standpoint, but because you appreciate your marvelous inheritance of divine qualities.

Remember that every time you talk depreciatingly of yourself, no matter if you do not really believe it, if you do it for effect, that is, telling others of your hard luck, admitting that you cannot get along as do other people, that you cannot make money and save it, that you don't seem to have any money sense, you are lowering your estimate of yourself, your ideal of yourself, and this is the pattern for your life building. There is a sculptor in you who is working to the pattern which you hold up to him, and if you hold up a defective, weak, deficient, dwarfed pattern, it will be built into the very structure of your being.

What you think of yourself will come to you; what you believe regarding yourself, your ability, your future, will tend to come to you. What you expect of yourself is this very instant being wrought into the texture of your being.

Always think of yourself as lucky. Never allow yourself to think of yourself in any other way. Say to yourself: "I am good luck. I must be lucky, because I am a part of the divinity which can never fail. I partake of omnipotence because I am a child of Omnipotence, a partner of the Almighty. It is my nature to be lucky. I was made to be lucky. I was born to win. I am the child of the King of kings. A princely inheritance is coming to me, and I must conduct myself with that respect for myself and for my ability which becomes a prince of the Most High."

Constantly meditate on what a marvelous

thing it is to have such an inheritance, to be conscious that you are really a god in the making, that there is a divinity within you which can never be lost, an omnipotence which can triumph over any handicap of earthly inheritance or accident.

Learn to reinforce yourself, to refresh and reinvigorate yourself by tapping the great cosmic intelligence through the subconscious mind, by going much into the silence and communing with the All-Good. You should no more harbor a fear thought, a worry thought, a jealousy, envy or hatred thought, a selfish thought, than you would listen to the temptation to steal. These things rob you of your peace of mind, your power, force and vitality, your poise as well as your comfort.

You would not allow a thief to ramble through your home to steal. Why should you allow your enemy thoughts to roam through your mind without a protest?

A dwarfed ideal means a dwarfed mind, a dwarfed future, a dwarfed career. Your conviction of yourself, your belief regarding yourself, your future, your ability, will all reappear in your career.

Someone says: "Dare to fling out into the great cosmic mind greater assurance about yourself; dare to have greater confidence; dare to believe in yourself and your mission. Have a grander ideal, a nobler aspiration."

A man must have faith in the thing he is trying to do or trying to get. His hope, his confidence, his expectation are powerful factors in the gaining of his ambition. They are searchlights on the horizon, descrying opportunity from afar.

Nothing can defeat you or rob you of success but *yourself*. No conditions, however inhospitable, can swamp you, or thwart your life aim—if you have a life aim. Your own weakness only can do that—your lack of determination, your lack of energy, your lack of backbone, your lack of confidence in yourself. Nothing in the world can make you a nonentity; no mischances, no conditions, no environment, nothing but yourself can do that. You can be a nobody if you will, or a somebody if you will; it is right up to you. You can make a success of your life; you can send your influence down the ages, or you can go to your grave a useless nobody, without ever having made a ripple in the current of the life of your day. Your luck, good or bad, is in yourself.

Thinking of your misfortune or hard luck in not being as well placed or as well conditioned as others is fatal to success and happiness, because we must go in the direction in which we face, and we face the way we think, the way we talk, the way we act. We are like weather vanes and we turn this way and that way according as we think. Our thoughts, our emotions, our feelings are like the wind which turns the weather vane.

I know of no one thing that will have a greater influence upon your life than the forming of the habit of thinking of yourself as lucky, regarding yourself as extremely fortunate in your birth, in your location, in your adaptation to your particular line of work, as fortunate in your ambition and in your chance in life to make good.

We are just beginning to learn that we are made, fashioned and molded by our thoughts, which are forces as real as is the force of electricity. Our thought is constantly shaping us to correspond with it. We are our own architects, our own sculptors. We are always reshaping, re-moulding ourselves to fit our thoughts and our emotions, our motives, our general attitude towards life. If we think of ourselves as being always lucky, we may not be extraordinary examples of good luck, but we shall always be happy, smiling and contented, believing that everything that comes to us is the best that we could possibly attain.

WHERE LUCK HAS BEEN FOUND

In thrift and foresight.

In thorough preparation for one's life work.

In mental alertness.

In always being ready to lend a helping hand wherever and whenever needed.

In being tactful and a good mixer.

In holding the efficiency ideal of oneself and one's capabilities.

In downright, constant hard work.

In being ready for the opportunity when it came.

In courtesy, kindness, and consideration toward everybody.

In helping oneself instead of looking to others for boosts, capital, or favors of any sort.

In doing one's work a little better than others did theirs.

In not being satisfied with anything but one's best, never accepting one's second best or a botched job.

In always carrying some reading matter in one's pocket, so that spare time could be utilized while waiting for trains, or for those who were tardy in appointments, by reading for self-improvement.

In being cheerful, no matter how dark the outlook.

In trying to make good in every possible way, while never taking advantage of others.

In beginning the thing which something within one said one could and ought to do, no matter what obstacles stood in the way; by obeying one's good impulses promptly, before they quit prodding one.

In never allowing oneself to believe that he was born to be poor, a failure, a mediocre sort of a man or woman.

In carrying the victorious attitude in everything, looking like a winner, talking like a winner, and radiating the confidence of a winner.

In holding that the good things of the world were not made for a favored few, but for all God's children.

In substituting clear grit and persistency for the advantages which many others enjoyed from birth.

In believing that the best part of one's salary was not in one's pay envelope but in the chance to make good in every bit of work that passed through one's hands.

In the opportunity to absorb the secrets of one's employer's business; to learn for pay what he bought dearly, perhaps, after failure and an enormous expenditure of money and time, and, possibly, the shortening of his life in the process.

In keeping eyes and ears open, and mouth closed most of the time.

In indomitable perseverance, a determination which knew no give up or retreat; in everlastingly pushing ahead whether one could see the goal or not.

In the right attitude towards life, towards one's work, towards everything and everybody.

In choosing one's company, associating

only with people who were doing their best to get on and get up in the world.

In the consciousness of one's partnership with the All-Good, the All-Supply, with the Infinite Mind.

In learning, through mental chemistry, to neutralize the things which kill one's best efforts—fear, worry, anxiety, jealousy, envy, malice, touchiness, anger, and thus to keep one's mind free for the larger things.

CHAPTER XIV

SELF-FAITH AND PROSPERITY

Faith unlocks the door to power.

It is the men and women with a stupendous faith, a colossal self-confidence, who do the great deeds, accomplish the "impossible."

No matter what your need is, put it into the hands of faith. Do not ask how, or why, or when. Just do your level best, and have faith, which is the great miracle worker of the ages.

Faith opens the door, sees the way. It is a soul sense, a spiritual foresight which peers far beyond the vision of the physical eyes and sees the reality long before it takes material form.

A one-talent man with an overmastering self-faith often accomplishes infinitely more than a ten-talent man who does not believe in himself.

Faith increases confidence, carries conviction, multiplies ability. It doesn't think or guess. It is not discouraged or blinded by mountains of difficulties, because it sees through them—sees the goal beyond.

There is a tremendous creative power in the conviction that we can do a thing.

You may succeed when others do not believe in you, when everybody else denounces you even, but never when you do not believe in yourself.

A COLOSSAL faith in himself, a sublime self-confidence that never wavered in any situation, was the great secret of Theodore Roosevelt's many-sided success, for he believed in Roosevelt, as Napoleon believed in Napoleon. There was nothing timid or half-hearted about him. He went at everything he undertook with that gigantic assurance, that tremendous confidence, that whole-hearted belief in his power to do the thing, that half wins the battle before it begins. Without any pretension to genius, as he himself said, with only the qualities of the average man, by intensive application he so developed every power of mind and body that he raised himself head and shoulders above the average man.

"According to thy faith be it unto thee," is just as scientific in the world of affairs as any demonstrated truth of science. Whether your ambition be to build up a great business, to accumulate a fortune, to win political power and influence, to make a great name in science, in politics, in journalism, in whatsoever field your bent inclines, a superb faith in yourself is the imperative price.

Most of the people in the great down-and-out army failed because they lacked faith in themselves. They doubted their power to make good. They did not believe enough in themselves, while they believed too much in circumstances and in help from other people. They waited for luck, waited for outside capital, for a boost, for influence, for a pull, for some one or something outside of them to help them. They depended too much upon everything else but themselves. And now they remain in the great failure army because they are not willing to pay the price for what they want, or they haven't the courage to try again. They lack that which faith gives—bulldog grit, tenacity, determination.

Self-confidence has ever been the best substitute for friends, pedigree, influence, and money. It is the best capital in the world; it has mastered more obstacles, overcome more difficulties, and carried through more enterprises than any other human quality. It has made more American millionaires than any other human force or quality.

It was the ambition to succeed, backed by the "I can and I will" spirit of self-confidence that enabled a poor boy, after repeated and disheartening failures, to give New York City its most beautiful business structure—the

Woolworth Building. Foreign architects have pronounced this one of the most beautiful in the world, "a dream in stone."

The man who brought it into being was Frank W. Woolworth. Born on a small farm in New York State, this man had no other heritage than a sound body and the native grit and self-reliance which have carried so many Americans to their goal. He began his career in a little grocery store, in the corner of a freight shed, owned by the station-master at Great Bend, N. Y. There he acted as grocery clerk and assistant station-master without pay. His first salary in a larger store was $3.50 a week. In spite of persistent hard work for years, disappointment and failures were the only visible results of his efforts. But in spite of hard luck and desperate poverty he hung on until fortune smiled, and then he began to establish the Woolworth five and ten cent stores, with the result that before his death, a few years ago, he had over a thousand stores with a capital of $65,000,000, giving employment to many thousands of people. He had also erected the great Woolworth Building, and, overtopping all, he had built a manly, lovable character. He left an example of honest success, wrung from the hardest conditions, that will be an inspiration to every youth who has an ambition to lift himself from poverty to power, while at the same time rendering great service to the world.

Henry Ford is another American who started in life with nothing but brain power and a belief in Henry's ability to do the thing he wanted to do. After many ups and downs, working first as a youth on the home farm near Detroit, later as a machinist, and as chief engineer of the Edison Illuminating Company, always plugging away in his spare time, developing the invention on which he began to work as a small boy, his farm tractor, he had passed the age of forty before he made acquaintance with success. Indeed, at forty he was supposed by those who could not gauge his character, his indomitable will, his faith in himself and his power to wring victory from defeat, to be a failure. But he was even then engaged in organizing the Ford Motor Company and well started on the way to the phenomenal success that has made his name known all over the world.

Now, at fifty-eight, Mr. Ford, many times a millionaire, is the head of an army of over 80,000 industrial workers, besides many others indirectly identified with his interests. He is owner of thirty-five manufacturing plants in the United States. The largest of these, which is at Highland Park, Detroit, employs 40,000 people in making Ford cars, while at the River Rouge plant, nine miles from Detroit, auto parts and tractors are turned out. He has a $5,000,000 tractor plant at Cork, Ireland, also assembling plants at Cadiz, Copenhagen, Bordeaux, and Manchester, England, and two in South America. In addition to all this, Mr. Ford owns *The Dearborn Independent,* a weekly publication, the Detroit, Toledo & Ironton Railroad, and a farm of 5,000 acres, west of Detroit, the food produce of which is sold to the employees of the Ford factories at cost prices. Nor is this industrial giant satisfied to stop here. His benevolent activities go hand in hand with his industrial achievements. His $5,000,000 hospital in Detroit, and his school for boys where they can "learn while they earn," are samples of what he is doing in this direction.

It is men of this type, men with one hundred per cent. of faith, who kill their doubts, strangle their fears, get up every time they fall and push to the front regardless of obstacles, who win out in life. As long as you live in an atmosphere saturated with failure thought you cannot do the biggest thing possible to you, because you cannot have a hundred per cent. of faith; and, remember, that your achievements, your success, will depend upon the percentage of your faith in yourself and in what you are trying to do.

A great many of those who fail in life, or who attain only mediocre positions, keep themselves back by self-depreciation, by a lack of faith in their own powers, the suggestion of their own inferiority. Nothing is more detrimental to success than this sort of mental attitude. It would take the stamina out of a Napoleon. The instant you acknowledge that you are incapable of doing the thing you attempt to do, or that anything can permanently block the way to the goal of your ambition, you set up a barrier to your success that no amount of hard work can remove. He can who thinks he can, holds true in every situation of life.

When some one asked Admiral Farragut if he were prepared for defeat, he said: "I certainly am not. Any man who is prepared for defeat would be half defeated before he commenced."

It makes a great difference whether you go into a thing to win, with clenched teeth and resolute will; whether you are prepared at the very outset to make your fortune, to succeed in your business or profession, to put through the thing you have set your heart on, or whether you start in with the idea that you will begin and work your way along gradually, and continue if you do not find too many obstacles, but that if all doesn't go well there is always a way to back out. To go into a thing determined to win, to feel that self-assurance, that inward sense of power that makes one master of the situation, is half the battle; while, on the other hand, to be prepared for defeat; to anticipate it is, just as Admiral Farragut said, to be half defeated before one commences. You must burn all your bridges behind you, leaving no temptation to retreat when things look black ahead.

The men who built up America's great industries and made enormous fortunes—the Peabodys, the Astors, the Goulds, the Vanderbilts, the Morgans, the Rockefellers, the Carnegies, the Schwabs, the Hills, the Fords, the Marshall Fields, the Wanamakers,—all the people who have done and are doing big things in the world,—not only had the faith which does the "impossible" but they have been exacting trainers of themselves. They do not handle themselves with gloves. They hold themselves right up to stern discipline. They do not allow dawdling, idling; they put a ban on laziness, indifference, vacillation; they fix their eye on the goal and sacrifice everything which interferes with their ambition, everything which stands in the way of the larger success. They know that he who is enamored of his easy chair, who thinks too much of his comfort and ease, his good times with his companions evenings, who thinks too much of the pleasures of the senses, will never get anywhere.

There is no possible way of defeating a human being who is victory organized. If he has the faith that moves mountains, if he has winning stuff in him, he is going to win, no matter what stands in the way. There is no holding him down, because, in addition to his unswerving belief in himself, he is ready to pay to the last cent the price that even the most gifted among men must pay for success. Nothing is denied to one who is willing to pay the price for it. Only your own inertia, your own lack of faith in yourself, your own lack of push and determination, can thwart your ambition. Your longings are the proofs that you can back them up with realities.

Faith makes light of obstacles, because it increases ability and multiplies power. Joan of Arc multiplied herself ten thousand times by her faith; multiplied her ability a million times by her conviction that she was God-ordained to restore the throne of France and drive the enemy from her soil. She was ready to make any sacrifice to save her country, and every sacrifice she made, every obstacle she overcame, made her stronger to accomplish the great task she had undertaken. Without work we know that faith is of no avail. Everything depends on the "hustle" with which we back it.

The only real power one ever gains is won in the struggle to overcome obstacles. It is the effort of brain and muscle put forth in the actual doing of the thing, the downright hard working, the vigorous thinking and planning that make the strong man, the man who reaches the goal of his ambition.

It was everlasting hustling, added to his indomitable self-confidence that made Alfred Harmsworth, now Lord Northcliffe, one of the wealthiest men in England, and one of the most successful publishers in the world. In an interview he said, "I feel that whatever position I have attained is due to focusing my energies and time. When I went into journalism I made up my mind that I would master the business of editing and publishing. This is a vast specialty, but then I was very young and had a good deal of self-confidence." This self-confidence was one of his most marked characteristics even as a boy. When only fifteen, while attending an English grammar school, he started a little school paper in which he said: "I have it on the best authority that this paper is to be a marked success." And a marked success it proved, as has every enterprise to which this hustling, self-confident journalist has put his hand. At twenty-one young Harmsworth started in the regular publishing business with a little weekly called "Answers," which was also a success. Before he had reached the age of thirty he was a millionaire publisher and at thirty-six he was the head of the largest publishing business in the world. Today Lord Northcliffe, who is regarded as one of the most powerful and influential men in England, is worth a great many million dollars, besides owning two million dollars' worth of paper-making timberland in Newfoundland.

We get in this life whatever we concentrate upon with all our might and main. Our success or failure is in our own hands. Many who are complaining that the door to success is locked and barred against them, because they are too poor to get an education, or they have no one to help them to get the position they desire, are not succeeding, are not getting the thing they want, because they are not willing to make the necessary effort to succeed. They are not willing to do the hard work, not willing to get right down on their marrow bones and hustle. They may have faith in their ability, but they haven't the energy to put the ability to work and make it do things for them. They want someone else to do the pushing, to make things happen for them. No man ever climbed to success on another's back. He must hustle, make things happen himself, or fail.

Joseph Pulitzer, a young boy who came to America from Germany, was so poor when he landed he had to sleep on the benches in City Hall Park, New York, in front of the space now occupied by the World Building, which he built later. This poor youth had so much faith and so much energy that he made millions out of a paper which was pretty nearly a failure in the hands of the people from whom he bought it.

No matter how humble your position, though you be but a section hand on a railroad, a street cleaner, a day laborer or a messenger boy, if you have faith in yourself, in your vision, and back up your faith with downright hard work, nothing can keep you from realizing your vision. A fortune is accumulated by the same means that make a man a successful musician, or politician, or inventor. Faith and work have magic in them. It is faith that leads the way in all undertakings. It is the divine faculty which connects men with the great Source of all supply, the Source of all intelligence, the Source of all power, of all possibilities. If you only have faith, one hundred per cent. faith in yourself, in your life work, in anything you undertake, you cannot fail.

THE GREAT CONQUEROR

I am that which is back of all achievement, which has led the way to success, to happiness, through the ages.

I crossed an unknown ocean with Columbus, who without me would never have discovered America.

I was with Washington at Valley Forge; and but for me he would not have succeeded in liberating the American colonies and making them a nation.

I went through the Civil War with Lincoln, and guided his pen when he wrote the Emancipation Proclamation that freed millions of human beings from slavery.

I was with the English patriots who forced

King John to sign that great charter of human rights—the Magna Charta.

I was back of those who forced the French Revolution—and of those who signed the American Declaration of Independence.

I was with Christ when all his disciples and friends had fled; and I cheered and comforted the martyrs at the stake—all the men and women who gave their lives to maintain the truths He taught.

I crossed the ocean with Cyrus W. Field fifty times before his great undertaking, the ocean cable, was perfected. I was on the ship with him when the cable parted in mid-ocean, after the first message had passed over it, and gave him courage to persist when the work had to be done all over again.

I am the locksmith who can unlock all doors, whom no obstacle can hold back, no difficulty or disaster dishearten, no misfortune swerve from my purpose.

I am a friend to the down-and-outs, the unfortunates, those to whom life has been a great disappointment. If these people would take hold of me I would turn them around so that they would face their goal and go toward it instead of turning their back on it and going in the opposite direction; they would face the sun and let the shadows fall behind instead of in front of them as in the past.

I am a booster, an optimist, one who always sees something of hope in every human being, for I know that there is a God in every one; that men and women are gods in the making; that they are all capable of doing infinitely more, infinitely better things, than they have yet done.

No matter how bad the conditions which confront me, I wear a smile, for I know that the sun is always behind the clouds and that after a time the storm will pass and the sun will shine again.

I see triumph beyond temporary defeat. I look past obstacles which discourage most people, for I know that they become smaller as one approaches them; and experience has shown me that but a very small fraction of the things which people dread, fear, and worry about ever happen.

If you know me, if you believe in me, work with me, cling to me, no matter how full of

failures and disappointments your past has
been, I will help you to overcome adverse conditions and crown you with success, for I conquer all difficulties.

I AM FAITH

CHAPTER XV

FEAR AND WORRY DEMAGNETIZE THE MIND:
HOW TO GET RID OF THEM

A day of worry is more exhausting than a week of work.

Fear impairs health, paralyzes efficiency, kills happiness, shortens life.

Crossing bridges before they come to them puts more victims in the great failure army, in the ranks of the unhappy and inefficient, than almost anything else. The fear of to-morrow, anticipation of the trials and troubles just ahead, robs multitudes of the strength and enthusiasm that would enable them to make to-day a glorious success.

The man who fears to-morrow is afraid of life, and that sort of man is a coward. He has no faith in God or in himself. He will never amount to much.

If you have had an unfortunate experience; if you have made a failure in your undertaking; if you have been placed in an embarrassing position; if you have fallen and hurt yourself by a false step; if you have been slandered and abused—forget it. There is not a single redeeming feature in these memories, and their ghosts will rob you of many a happy hour.

It is not the work we have actually done, the burdens we have actually borne, the troubles that have actually come that have furrowed deep wrinkles in the faces of many of us, and made us prematurely old; it is the useless fears and worries we have lugged along with us that have done all the mischief.

DR. WILLIAM F. WARREN, a former president of Boston University, in an address to the students said: "No command or entreaty occurs so many times in the Bible as this emphatic one, 'Fear not!' I once thought to prepare a sermon on it, but it proved too fruitful for me. From Genesis to Apocalypse 'Fear not' seemed an unending refrain. I began to count the occurrences; soon I had twenty, then thirty, then forty, then fifty. Glancing from fifty to seventy I noticed that other words, like those of our Lord, 'Let not your heart be troubled, neither let it be afraid,' meant exactly the same thing; so that my count, however complete, never represents the true total."

Yet there are millions of people in America, in every part of the world, whose minds are constantly filled with the fear of something. From the cradle to the grave, fear throws its black shadow over mankind, marring and stunting vast multitudes of lives, making people wretched, keeping them in poverty and inferiority, driving many to insanity and death.

Not long ago a girl in New York slipped on an icy pavement and fell to the street. At the moment an approaching truck passed so close to her that the wheels almost touched her. Terror-stricken at the thought of her danger, the girl imagined that the horses and the truck had actually passed over her. When picked from the street and taken to a nearby hospital in an ambulance she was raving about the horses and the truck running over her, and finally became insane.

This tragedy was purely the result of imagination, for there was not a scratch of any kind on the girl's body, not even her clothes having been touched. Like the fears and worries that makes the lives of so many people wretched failures, the thing that drove away her reason had no reality. The thing she feared never happened, but the effect of her fear, the conjuring up in her mind a picture of death, or of a multilated body, brought upon her something worse, something more disastrous; for no other loss can compare with the blotting out of the light of reason.

The wrong kind of thought is daily bringing disaster, frightful tragedies and misfortunes into the lives of men and women everywhere. A short time ago during a severe thunderstorm, a woman became unconscious from fright and died. An examination showed that there was no heart trouble, and that the light-

ning had not touched her; but it appeared that
all her life the woman had felt a great nervous
dread of thunder and lightning, and finally the
thing she had long feared and expected came
to her. It was not the lightning, however, but
her fear of it that had killed her.

Multitudes to-day are seriously affected
through fear of disease. They fear and expect influenza or pneumonia, and so invite
these diseases. Their fear destroys their dis-
ease-resisting power and predisposes them to
become victims. We had a striking example
of this soon after America entered the World
War, when the influenza epidemic made its appearance in the soldiers' camps, and then
spread through the country like wildfire. In
an incredibly short time, thousands of victims, mostly young people, were carried off
by the dread disease. Fear was at the bottom
of its widespread destructiveness.

Through the influence of the fear thought,
the gloomy, discouraged thought, the disease
thought, the failure thought,—all sorts of morbid thoughts and imaginings—people are cutting off their divine supply, ruining their
health, their possibilities of success and happi-

ness. The fear of death, the fear of disease, the fear of coming to want, the fear of failure, the fear of what our neighbors will think and say, the fear of accidents, anticipating misfortunes, bad luck generally, the fear of the future, of the miscarriage of our plans, fear of this, fear of that and the other, makes this, the most negative and destructive of all human emotions, the closest companion of our daily lives. Fear is the damnable ghost that is always bobbing up to rob us of our legitimate enjoyment, of our peace of mind, of our courage and strength, of our faith in ourselves and our ability to rise above conditions that cramp and hold us in thrall.

Take the fear of poverty alone. Consider the misery it has caused. Who can ever estimate what havoc this single fear has played in the race history,—the fear of coming to want, the torture of visualizing the wolf approaching the door; the agony of possible suffering for our loved ones if we cannot provide for their needs! Oh, this terrible fear of want! We read it in the faces of multitudes of people who never have learned to demonstrate supply, who know nothing of the law of prosperity and never dream that holding in mind this fear of want, this horror of poverty, having the conviction that they are doomed to be poor all their lives, is driving away from them the supply, the opulence they long for. They do not know that it is only by holding the prosperity thought, the thought of abundance; by picturing themselves in connection with limitless supply, visualizing what they want instead of what they don't want, that they will get away from the poverty they hate and connect with the very fountainhead of supply.

How many men and women deplete their strength and thus lessen their earning power by lying awake nights worrying over their business problems, their home problems, the expanding needs of their growing families, and wondering where their supply is coming from! Has this fear and worry business ever done anything for you? Has it ever added to your income, to your health, to your comfort or your happiness? Has it ever solved your problems or helped you in any way? Hasn't it always done just the reverse? Most of us know from bitter experience how the vicious fear and worry habit uses up our mental powers, saps our life forces, cuts down our efficiency, robs us of hope, courage, and enthusiasm; in fact, cuts down our success chances fully seventy-five per cent.

The great secret of success, and of happiness, too, is to have faith; to face life with courage and confidence, and not to anticipate trouble. It is greatly to our discredit that, in spite of the fact that America is the richest, the most prosperous, the most productive and resourceful country in the world, we are a nation of worriers. The majority of us don't face life in the right way; we fear and worry more than any other people on earth. The Public Health Service in Washington realizing this, and knowing the evil effects of such a mental attitude in breeding nervous diseases and other life stranglers, some time ago issued a bulletin, the burden of which was, "Don't worry." "So far as is known," it said, "no bird ever tried to build more nests than its neighbor. No fox ever fretted because he had only one hole in which to hide. No squirrel ever died of anxiety lest he should not lay by enough nuts for two winters instead of for one, and no dog ever lost any sleep over the fact that he did not have enough bones laid aside for his declining years."

In other words, we might take a lesson from what we call the "lower animals" in not worrying about our future supply, which is one of the chief sources of our anxiety. We say they cannot reason, but they show far more intelligence in this matter than we do; they show that faith we lack, that faith which the Christ so constantly tried to implant in his disciples: "Therefore take no thought [that is, no anxious thought] saying what shall we eat? or What shall we drink? or, Wherewithal shall we be clothed? . . . For your heavenly Father knoweth that ye have need of all these things. . . . Take therefore no thought for the morrow; for the morrow shall take thought for the things of itself. Sufficient unto the day is the evil thereof."

Rich and poor alike are victims of the unreasonable fear of lack of supply, lack of means, as all panics and business depressions show, for it is the wealthy who through withdrawal of cash from business and banks, first disturb public credit. Of course not all of us anticipate financial shortages. There are many who, though not what the world calls wealthy, do not worry over money matters: instead they allow fear and worry to get hold of them through some other obsession, the anticipation of failure in their work, a breakdown in their health, some misfortune to their children, the fear that some member of the family may go wrong, bring disgrace upon themselves and all connected with them.

Now, the man or the woman who is constantly afraid of some impending evil, always dreading, anticipating something that will work to his or her injury, or who is worrying about something that has already happened, is lacking in the most essential character and success elements—courage, self-confidence, and faith in the divine God-power in the great within of man, which makes him greater than anything that can happen to him. Such a fear-stricken, worrying soul shows by his mental attitude that he does not believe in God; that he is not anchored in the consciousness of the limitless power and resources that are at his command; that he lacks confidence in the infinite Power that creates, preserves, and upholds the universe.

Don't be one of those craven souls; don't allow yourself to be robbed of your birthright—success and happiness. Even if you have the fear and worry habit, you can free yourself from it. Professor William James says that fear is conquerable; that it has at last become possible for large numbers of people to pass from the cradle to the grave without ever having a pang of genuine fear. There is no doubt that fear and worry, those terrible evils that have so long cursed mankind and held back the development of the race can be absolutely driven out of our lives. And you will not get very far, my friend, nor climb very high, until you rid yourself of your fears and doubts, of the worry and discouragement which are blighting your life, strangling your aspirations and obscuring your ideals. How many really able people are struggling along, barely making a living, getting nowhere near the realization of their youthful dreams, because they listened to the whisperings of those human traitors, the fears and doubts and worries which held them back from doing what they were sent into the world to do!

It is for you to determine *now* whether

you shall continue to be the slave of fear and worry; to lead the narrow, pinched life, limited in all its possibilities and power of expression, that you have so long been living, or whether you shall leave it forever behind you and rise to the height of your divine power and possible achievement through claiming your kinship with God—with whom all things are possible. You don't need to make any preparations, to delay for anything, or to ask anyone's assistance. You can break away from your discouraging past; you can change your poverty-stricken environment and plant your feet firmly in the path of attainment; you can do this *instantly* by reversing your thought. Through the exercise of your divine power you can change your thought at will; and to change the thought is the first step in the cure of any evil condition.

Worry, anxiety, lack of faith, self-depreciation, timidity, lack of self-confidence, these are all expressions of fear, and cannot exist in your mind for a moment in the presence of the courage, thought, the mental suggestion of fearlessness, self-confidence, self-reliance; the image of yourself as strong, resourceful, courageous, in touch with the infinite reservoir of divine power and energy that flows to you from your Source, the Omnipotent One, the Creator of the universe. Instead of picturing trouble and misfortune ahead, brooding over the difficulties that confront you, and fearing you will never be able to get past them, flood your mind with triumphant thoughts, with the thought of the power that is stored in the great within of you, always wanting to be used, always more than a match for the giant fear that tries to frighten you with bogies, with unrealities that have no existence outside of your troubled imagination.

No fear, no anxiety, no discouragement, no doubt or apprehension regarding the future, can possibly enter your mind while it is filled with thoughts of hope, of courage, of assurance, of all power and strength through your connection with Infinite Power.

You will find it a great help in driving out fear and worry to express strong, courageous sentiments aloud. When alone say to any enemy thoughts that would frighten or harass you: "Get out of my mental kingdom. I will not allow you to come between me and my

Father. I am a son of God, and I was never made to cower before anything; to be frightened and turned from my purpose by a mere thought. I am brave, courageous, afraid of nothing; I am a conqueror of fear, not its slave."

Remember, that as God's child you have nothing to fear, for through your kinship with Omnipotence, the Source of all courage, of all supply, of all beauty, of all good, no evil thing has power over you. The next time that something which you feel is holding you back whispers to you, "Don't do that; you'll make a fool of yourself. Many a stronger, abler man than you are has failed in trying to do that same thing. Many with more ability, in more favorable circumstances, with more influence, and with outside help, have failed in the ambitious undertaking you are going to attempt, poor and ill-equipped as you are. You had better be careful; make sure that you are going to succeed before you begin,"—don't listen to the evil thing, for it is fear that is whispering to you. And it is lying as it has lied to millions who came before you, as it will lie to millions who come after you. He who listens to it will never enter into his heritage as a child of God, his birthright of peace, power, harmony, success, abundance.

Fear and doubt, discouragement and worry are always found together. They belong to the same family, and work for the same end—to rob people of energy and ambition, and to keep them from doing what they were made to do. They have ever been the great retarders of human progress, the great killers of ability, the blighters of happiness, the stranglers of aspirations, the murderers of success. They have kept untold millions in mediocrity and have caused utter failure and ruin of other millions who could have done big things had they gone ahead, made the most of their ability and worked steadily for the realization of their early visions. God never meant any of His children to be victims of fear, worry, discouragement or any evil specter of the imagination. He intended that their lives should be triumphant achievements, glorious successes, and not miserable failures.

Whatever tries to hold you back from the pursuit of a high ambition is your enemy. When fear tries to shake your confidence in yourself, to keep you from beginning the things which you long to do and feel that you have the ability to carry through; when you feel yourself weakening before some unusual difficulty and think of turning back; when you are tempted to worry about something that has happened, or that you think may happen; when you doubt your ability to do this or that, and think you would better not undertake anything that is not perfectly sure to come out all right, drive all such suggestions out of your mind. Asserting your divine power as a son of God, say to yourself: "Now, it is right up to me to make good. I can't give up this way and turn coward. It would be unmanly, contemptible. I am able to overcome this thing; it has no power to keep me down. No matter whether I can see the way or not I shall keep going, forging ahead. No matter what obstacles may come up I shall keep headed toward the port of my ambition. Nothing has power over me, but what I give it. I will not allow anything to thwart my purpose and destroy my career. I can and I will rise above all my troubles, above all my mistakes and errors. Nothing can keep me from my own, for from now on I will work with the God in me. I will not be overcome by any enemy; I will overcome."

Nothing but ourselves can make God's promise to man void,—"Behold I have set before you an open door which no man can shut." The door that leads to your ambition, to the fuller, happier, more abundant life you desire is wide open. No one can close it but yourself. Nothing but your doubts, your fears, your pessimism, your worry, your lack of faith in the Creator and in yourself can prevent you from matching your desires with reality.

CHAPTER XVI

GOOD CHEER AND PROSPERITY

Smiles attract dollars as they attract everything that is good and wholesome.

The man who keeps his machinery well lubricated with love, good-will and good cheer can withstand the hard jolts and disappointments of life infinitely better than the man who always looks on the dark side.

"No smiles, no business."

Good cheer is one of man's greatest benefactors. It has helped him from giving up to despair even when starvation has stared him in the face and all mankind seemed against him.

When a man chooses good cheer for his companion he never talks of hard times or carries a picture of poverty or want in his mind.

The cheerful man is pre-eminently the useful man.

IF I were asked to name the one thing that would help the human race more than any other, I would perhaps say, "More cheerfulness,—good cheer, keeping sweet under all circumstances."

More cheerfulness means more life, more happiness, more success, more efficiency, more character, a larger future. The cheerful man does not cramp his mind and take half views of things.

Have you never noticed that, as a rule, it is the cheerful, hopeful, optimistic people who succeed, and that it is the sour, morose, gloomy natures who fail or plod along in mediocrity, who never amount to anything? A habit of cheerfulness enables one to transmute apparent misfortunes into real blessings.

More cheerfulness will help you all along the line of life. It will help you to bear your burdens; it will help you to overcome obstacles; it will increase your courage, strengthen your initiative, make you more effective, more popular, more helpful. It will make you a happier, more successful man or woman; it will transform and beautify the humblest and homeliest surroundings.

Cheerfulness means poise, serenity, a sane, wholesome, well-balanced outlook on life. The cheerful man knows that there is much misery, but that misery need not be the rule of life. There is no philosophy like cheerfulness. No one can estimate the healthful, uplifting power of one cheerful life, one serene, balanced soul. The hopeful, cheerful nature is constructive. He who has formed a habit of looking at the bright side of things has a great advantage over the chronic dyspeptic who sees no good in anything.

Shakespeare says:

"A merry heart goes all the day,
Your sad tires in a mile—a"

There is no other life habit which can give such prolific returns in happiness and satisfaction as that of being cheerful and sweet under all circumstances. The cheerful man's thought sculptures his face into beauty and touches his manner with grace. Why not resolve that, whatever comes or does not come to you, whether you fail in your undertaking or succeed, you will keep cheerful, hopeful, optimistic, and be grateful for the good things that are yours? In almost everything we can find some happiness if we look for it. The trouble with us is that we generally want more to make us happy than we deserve, and we are not grateful enough for the many things that are ours to enjoy.

How many of us might learn a lesson from

the poor little girl living in the slums of a great city who took a prize at a flower show. When asked how she managed to raise her beautiful plant in the dark alley where her home was, she answered that there was a little space between two tall buildings through which a bit of sunshine came in, and that by moving the plant as the sun moved she had managed to keep it in the sunshine and to produce the prize flower. We all have at least a little sunshine in our lives, something to be thankful for, and by turning our faces to it, we could manage somehow to keep growing, but we don't make the most of the little sun we do have, as the little girl did.

There is much that even the poorest of us might enjoy in the common, everyday life, if we would only now and then stop, look, listen, think and contemplate; if we would only try to see things in their true light, to hear the voices of Nature, to see the miracles going on about us on every hand in God's great laboratory. We could be happy in the most ordinary situations in life if we would only learn to delve down into the common things, to appreciate them, to see their marvelous beauty.

But no, it is always what we want, not what we have, that claims our attention. It's the far-away thing, it's to-morrow, next year, when we are better off, when we are a little better able to have luxuries, to have an automobile, to travel, then we'll enjoy ourselves and have a good time.

I know a man who, although very poor, can manage to get more comfort out of a real tough, discouraging situation than any one else I have ever known. I have often seen him when he did not have a dollar to his name, with a wife to support, yet he was always buoyant, happy, cheerful, contented. He would even make fun out of an embarrassing situation, see something ludicrous in his poverty. He never was in a difficulty that blotted out the sun for him, for he always saw light ahead; and there is no doubt in my mind but that ultimately he will be a big success in his business.

If we are cheerful and contented all nature smiles with us; the air is balmier, the sky clearer, the earth has a brighter green, the trees have a richer foliage, the flowers are more fragrant, the birds sing more sweetly, and the sun, moon and stars are more beautiful.

Money itself has very little to do with happiness. Some of the most wretched men and women I have ever known anything about have been very rich. They could have everything that money could buy, but their money didn't bring them happiness; it didn't bring contentment or harmony into their homes. In fact, if many of these men and women had been poor, they would have been infinitely happier.

High-minded cheerfulness is found in great souls, self-poised and confident in their own heaven-aided powers.

Epictetus, the pagan philosopher, proved in his life the truth of his own words—"A man can be happy without wealth, without family, without office or honor, without health, without anything that the world seeks after." There are few of us lacking in all these things, but we are not happy because we are not normal as Epictetus was.

Multitudes of people think that happiness consists largely in getting rid of disagreeable things, disagreeable duties, in getting rid of the dry, dreary, routine of life, the compulsory drudgery: in getting rid of the responsibility of providing ways and means. They think they would be happy if they could only get freedom from the irksome things of life, the pinching, the hitching along from day to day, which comes from trying to do business on limited capital; freedom from duns, frets, and naggings; freedom from the thousand and one pricks and annoyances of the daily workaday life. In short, most of us think we would surely be happy if we were released from the anxiety of the bread-and-butter question; if we did not have to think about the cost of things or the ways and means of getting them.

But, as far as we know, rich people are no happier than poor people. With them it is largely a question of shifting anxiety and worry to other things. The moment people get beyond the necessity of working, beyond anxiety about the cost of living, there are many other enemies of their happiness to creep into their lives and destroy their harmony—if they allow them.

The things which torment us, which keep us from being cheerful and happy are the boomerangs that come back to us from our wrong doing; all the mental wounds from which we suffer are self-inflicted. No human being can possibly injure another without injuring himself more. He cannot do wrong without paying for it in corresponding suffering. In a similar way our thoughts react upon our prosperity and happiness.

The new philosophy shows us that we do not have to die to come to our own, to reach our heaven, the heaven of our dreams, that the grave is not the portal of paradise, but that paradise is here and we are living in paradise but don't know it, because we can't see it, except as we get a glimpse of heaven shining through in all that is beautiful and sweet and lovely and kindly. It teaches us that paradise is gained by right living and right thinking, right acting, by practicing the God qualities. It teaches us that we can never awake in His likeness until we practice His qualities, the qualities which make up divinity. It teaches us that our consciousness of our oneness with the One is the source of all our strength, the source of all our power, the secret of all our success that is worth while, the source of our healing.

The new philosophy teaches us to face toward the light whether we can see the goal or not, always to look in the hopeful direction. It teaches us to look toward success, toward opulence, toward prosperity, no matter how poverty-stricken our environment seems. It teaches us to look toward the perfect man that God planned, that God intended, not to see the sick or the diseased or the immoral, sinful, criminal or defective man. It teaches us that when we look at human beings through suspicious eyes, through distrusting eyes, through doubting eyes, through envious, jealous, or hatred eyes, we arouse in them, by an inevitable law, the very qualities which we hold in our mind, the qualities which we see in them. If we wish to appeal to the best, if we wish to draw the best out of others, we must look for the best in them; we must think the best of them; we must trust them; we must believe in them.

The man who smiles and sees the best in everything and everybody is the man who draws the best out of others. He attracts others and wins out in life, while the gloomy, sour face repels everyone.

"No smiles, no business," is the motto of a successful business house. At first this struck me as rather a peculiar motto, but on second thought, I realized how apt it is. Do we not all know that sour, gloomy faces drive away business, and that pleasant, sunny faces attract it? Cheerfulness will attract more customers, sell more goods, do more business with less wear and tear than any other quality.

Nobody but himself may be helped by the money millionaire, but everybody is enriched who knows or comes in contact with the millionaire of good cheer, and the more he gives of his wealth the more it multiplies.

Andrew Carnegie owed his popularity and much of his success and happiness to his cheerful disposition. In his later years he said: "My young partners do the work and I do the laughing, and I commend to you the thought that there is very little success where there is little laughter."

Whoever strikes the keynote of joy and happiness is a dispenser of the balm of Gilead, of a healing force. A man without cheerfulness is a sick man. The sadness of his spirit lays a withering blight on all the beauty of his life. He becomes prematurely old. His strength decays. "A broken spirit drieth up the bones."

But cheerfulness is a medicine. It promotes health. The habit of cheerfulness lubricates the human machine and very greatly increases and sharpens every one of the mental faculties. It improves every function of the body. Cheerfulness keeps one young; it is one of the secrets of eternal youth.

One who admits to himself and others that he is sick is indeed sick; but one who declines to make such admission, and cheerfully goes on as if he were well, conquers many an ailment, which if he had succumbed to it, might have proved serious.

Beecher used to speak of sunny natures who moved through the world like cheering music, spreading joy and gladness wherever they went. We have all met rare souls who live in the sunlight all the time. No matter how poor they may be in worldly goods they see something in life to be thankful for. They are always helpful, hopeful, encouraging, happy. Wherever they go they scatter sunshine.

If we cannot always so control our moods as to be really happy we can always appear cheerful. This is a duty we owe ourselves and society. It is weak and cheap to go about radiating mental poison, the poison of discouragement, of gloom; the poison of worry and anxiety. It is weak to go about the world wearing mourning in our expression. It is a sin to peddle gloom and despondency. We owe it to the world and to ourselves to scatter sunshine, to appear at our best, not at our worst.

There is significance in the fact that man is the only animal that has a sense of humor—that can laugh. The Creator meant us to have fun; to rejoice and be glad always. Happiness is man's birthright. Laughter is a token of saneness. Abnormal people, insane people, seldom laugh. It is as natural to a normal human being to want to laugh and have a good time as it is to breathe. There is something wrong about a person who never laughs, who is always serious. Things which amuse and make us enjoy life have a healthful physical and moral influence.

The happiness habit is just as necessary to our best welfare, to any success that is worth the name, as the work habit, or the honesty habit, or the square-dealing habit. We can cultivate the habit of being cheerful and happy just as we can cultivate the habit of being polite to every one with whom we come in contact.

Anything that will make a man feel joyous and happy, that will clear the cobwebs of discouragement from his brain and drive away fear, care, and worry, is of practical value and should be encouraged. Innocent, hearty fun will do this as nothing else can.

It is the shrewdest kind of business policy to do what will recreate, refreshen, and rejuvenate one for the next day's work. Then why not have a lot of fun and laughter in the home?

One of the greatest sins multitudes of parents commit against their children is suppressing their love of play in the home. Many parents insist that their children must not talk or laugh at meals. This is a crime against childhood. It is actually unfitting them to be pleasant and agreeable companions, "good mixers" when they grow up and go out in the world, for the habits of childhood become a part of the grown man and woman.

Fun is as necessary as bread. He makes a mistake who regards laughter and humor as transitory, superficial things that pass away and leave nothing behind. They have a permanent, beneficial influence on the whole character and career.

Having a good time should be a part of our daily program. Why should this not enter into our life-plan? Why should we be serious and gloomy over our work, over our meals? Why not do everything with joy and gladness?

Cheerfulness will help you all along the line of life. It will help you bear your burdens; it will help you to overcome obstacles; it will increase your courage, strengthen your initiative and make you more effective. It will not only make you a happier, but also a more successful and progressive man. Cheerfulness, more joy in the life, is our greatest need.

Struggles, disappointments, difficulties are not meant to make us sad, but to make us strong—for if we do not whine and complain, we shall be given strength to overcome all these.

The cheerful man sees that everywhere the good outbalances the bad, and that every evil has its compensating balm.

Robert Louis Stevenson said, "A happy man or woman is a better thing to find than a five-pound note. He or she is a radiating focus of good will and their entrance into a room is as though another candle had been lighted."

We were all made for happiness, to rejoice and be exceeding glad. Any inharmony or discord in our nature is contrary to divine law and divine will. It was the Creator's intention that everybody should be happier than the happiest beings are to-day.

If you, my friend, have not found that source of happiness which will keep you in poise and serenity, no matter what may happen to you or yours, if you have not found that poise which gives the peace that passeth understanding under all conditions, you have not yet found the great secret of life. You have yet to learn that real enjoyment, real satisfaction does not come from the possession of things, does not come from outside sources, but that our highest satisfaction, our highest enjoyment, our highest happiness, ever comes from within. Here is the fountain of all supply; here is where we touch God, the Source of all good; here is where we tap the divinity in the great within of us.

If your supply is limited and you feel unhappy, dissatisfied, gloomy, you may be sure that there is something wrong inside of you. There is something wrong in your thought, in your motive, in your acts, something wrong in your view of life. You are violating your nature in some way or you are not using your powers rightly.

CHAPTER XVII

THE MASTER KEY—TO BE GREAT, CONCENTRATE

Two friends set out on a journey once, oh, many years ago,
The one bestrode a mettled steed, the other trudged below;
And he that rode raced everywhere, save to the place he should,
"Because," said he, "there's time enough, and this, my mount,
   is good."
Time journeyed, too, and when, at last, the limit's hour did toll,
The one that pleasure's bubble sought was still far from the
   goal,
While he that came with tedious pace was at his travel's end,
With but one shadow on his heart,—the failure of his friend.
                   T. H. Winton.

THE son of a poor Welsh schoolmaster, without advantage of birth or fortune, without pull or influence of any kind, David Lloyd George succeeded in raising himself to the highest position in the British Empire. As Prime Minister of England, he ranks next to King George, while his power and responsibility greatly overtop that of the King or any other man in the empire.

What is the secret of his success? One word tells it: concentration.

Before the boy was two years old, his father

227

died.   His mother then took her family to live
with her brother, Richard Lloyd, a humble
cobbler.   The cobbler's shop was a sort of political forum for workingmen of the neighborhood, and there young David got his early
training in politics.   In his teens he studied
law, and at the age of twenty-one began to
practice.   But long before he was admitted
to the bar, when he first visited the House of
Commons, he made up his mind that that was
to be his future domain, and then and there resolved to enter parliament.   With all the vigor
and tenacity of his nature he concentrated on
his ambition, with what result the world knows.
One of the ablest and most brilliant statesmen
England has produced, he is to-day the most
dominant figure in world affairs.

What David Lloyd George has done in his
field you can do in yours, as millions of others
have done, by the same means,—concentration.

There is no more powerful magnet in the
world for attracting the thing we desire, no
force more effective in realizing the ambition
we long to attain than concentration.   It has
been the chief factor in all the great achieve-

ments of history. It is the cornerstone of success in every line; the principle upon which all progress is based. All the inventions, all the discoveries, all the modern facilities which the world enjoys are the children of focused minds. Whatever you long to be, or to have, you can be, you can have, by focusing your mind and concentrating your efforts on that one thing.

When Franz Liszt, the great composer, was a mere youth, his elder brother chided him for spending his time on music and told him that he himself was going to be a great landowner. The would-be landowner scorned his young brother's musical bent, holding that a talent for music would only ruin a man. Franz, however, stuck to his bent, and even ran away several times in order to gratify the ambition for a musical career, which was discouraged at home.

Years later when the elder brother had become a wealthy landowner he called on Franz, who was still a struggling musician. Not finding him at home he left his card which bore the inscription, "Herr Liszt, Landowner." When more years had passed and the young composer had finally won out, he returned the call of his landowner brother and presented his card, which read, "Herr Liszt, Brain-owner."

Aside from the humor of this little story, the point is, that each of the brothers got what he concentrated on; the one became a wealthy landowner, the other a world-famed musician and composer.

If your ambition is like that of the elder brother, to become a wealthy landowner, a prosperous man of affairs, then you must concentrate on prosperity, on the acquisition of wealth in some form. We all know men who seem to attract money from every direction. Everything they touch turns to money, as we say, while others who work just as hard for the same end have no success at all. The different results are due to the difference in intensity and persistence of concentration. The natural, the born money-maker thinks in terms of money; he is making money mentally all the time, so to speak, because his mind is focused on money. He is always nursing his money vision. He is positive in his conviction that he will make money, will be wealthy, and he concentrates on his object with such intensity and singleness of aim that he literally creates money.

The man who wants money, but who doesn't concentrate intensely on getting it; who doesn't believe very much in his ability to get it, who fears he will never be even what we call a well-to-do man, is like one who wants to be successful, but is always thinking about failure, worrying about it, fearing, believing, that he never will become a success. Or like a man of average ability who should scatter his forces in a dozen different directions, hoping that by chance he might manage to succeed in some one of them.

There is no such thing as succeeding in anything by chance. The greatest genius in the world never created a masterpiece in any line —by chance. Concentration is the master key to all success. It is the fundamental law of achievement. The man who does not concentrate will be either a half success, a mediocrity, or a complete failure.

The French have a proverb, "He who does one thing is terrible." In other words, he who sticks to one thing is irresistible. No matter if a world opposed his progress he would forge his way through to his goal. It was bending all his energies to the accomplishment of his purpose that made Napoleon one of the most notable figures in history. His intense concentration on his one unwavering aim enabled him to write his name on the very stones of the capital of France; to stamp it indelibly upon the heart of every Frenchman. Even to-day, a century after his death, France, though a republic, is still under the spell of Napoleon's name.

"To make a success of the shoe business is my one great ambition," said the head of one of the largest shoe houses in the world not long ago. "I am not a director or trustee of any bank. I do not scatter my energies. I don't pretend to know many things, but I do know something about the shoe business. *I have put my ability, my energy, my life into the work of making good shoes.*"

This man, who began life on the lowest round of the ladder, without capital or influence, built up a business which keeps a force of two hundred traveling salesmen on the road to-day and is turning over some $25,000,000 a year.

Emerson says, "The one prudence in life is concentration; the one evil is dissipation." Scattering our energies, dissipating our creative force, failing to bring our mind to a focus and to hold it there, is responsible for nine-tenths of the failures in life and most of the poverty of the world. I know one of those dissipators who generates more new ideas and outlines more new schemes than anyone else I have ever met. Yet he has never accomplished anything more than the making of a meager living, because he never sticks long enough to any one thing to make it go. His brain power and all of his energy are scattered in following one new thing after another without ever carrying any of them forward to completion. Every time I talk with him he amazes me with the fertility of his mind, his resourcefulness in developing original ideas, many of which would prove valuable if they were only put into execution, but they never get beyond the mental stage. The concentration necessary to bring them down to earth, to put them to work, is lacking. There are thousands like this man, getting small salaries in very ordinary positions, whose knowledge of a dozen different occupations, concentrated in one line, would have made them efficient specialists. Everywhere we find men who early in life studied law, medicine, theology, who taught school a few years, worked in a store a little, took a hand at railroading, did a little business, traveled for some house, and finally settled down at one thing, only to find that their training years, the years of largest opportunity, when they were susceptible to discipline, had gone by.

No matter how brilliant or versatile you may be you cannot afford to divide your ability, to throw away valuable experience in jumping from one vocation to another. If you would succeed in a worth-while way, you must be a whole man with undivided interests, able to fling the weight of your entire being into one calling. No one is large enough to be split up into many parts; and the sooner a man can stamp this truth upon his mind the better his chances for being a profitable member of society.

Elbert Hubbard says: "The master man is a person who has evolved intelligent industry, concentration, self-confidence until these things become the habit of his life."

Coleman Dupont furnished a good example of the master-man at a critical stage in the affairs of the Dupont Powder Company. When he was called to the head of the business it was losing ground rapidly, but through his amazing industry and concentration, backed by confidence in his ability to do what he undertook, he very soon turned the tide and headed the company toward success. When an interviewer asked Mr. Dupont how he did this, he said: "I talked powder, I ate powder, I dreamed powder. I thought of little else but powder." This concentration on one unwavering aim built up an enormous institution of world-wide fame.

No matter what your business, trade, or profession, you cannot make a mistake in following Mr. Dupont's remarkable methods of concentration which make him a master-man in his line. Think the thing you want; talk it; live it; breathe it; dream it; act it; radiate it from every pore of your body; saturate your life with it; visualize it; believe that it is already yours. That's the only way to get anything of value in this world. If we could only realize the marvelous power of thought, the creative force in concentration, the drawing power of intense visualizing, how much more we could accomplish! It is this which really makes the mind a powerful magnet to attract what it desires, what it longs for most. Everywhere we see illustrations of the attractive force of positive, definite thought concentrated on one point.

Take the little Hebrew boys who come from other countries to America when very young. From the start they have the concentrated commercial instinct of their race. They think in terms of money making; they keep their minds on ways and means of making money until they become powerful magnets, attracting money from every direction. That's why they succeed and become wealthy where American youths with far better opportunities attract poverty and remain poor all their lives. From the time the Hebrew boy starts to shine shoes on the street, to sell papers, or to peddle some small articles, he is all the time thinking of the money he is going to make; counting what he has and planning what he will do with it; how he can increase it; how he can enlarge his little business, put his profits to work for him and accumulate more money. In a very short time he has a newsstand or a little shop of his own; he invests in a little real estate; by and by he borrows some money and puts up a house, and so he goes on trading in one thing and another, his mind always bent on making more money, until one day this little newsboy, or bootblack, or peddler becomes a man of fortune, a millionaire.

To demonstrate prosperity, you must concentrate on prosperity; you must hold the prosperity attitude; to demonstrate abundance, you must think abundance, just as you must think health, think vigor, if you would be healthy and vigorous. It is not enough to long for health; you must believe that you will be, that you already are, well and strong. You must expect it. According to thy faith be it unto thee. You must hold in mind that thing, whatever it is, you wish to express in your life, and you must believe it will come. The student who is trying to become a lawyer saturates his mind with law. He thinks law, reads law, studies law, keeps his mind focused upon a future as a lawyer; keeps in a law atmosphere; he pictures himself practising at the bar, a man of mark in his profession; he continually fills his life with the law ideal, and by the force of his powerful concentration fits himself for the practice of law.

The medical student must follow the same method; so must the aspirant to the ministry or any other vocation. And so must the aspirant to wealth.

You can't expect to become prosperous if you don't hold fast to the prosperity vision, if you don't believe with all your heart you are going to be prosperous. If your mind is occupied with something else most of the time; if it is filled with doubts about ever accumulating property or becoming prosperous in any line of business, don't deceive yourself with the idea that prosperity will come to you if you only work hard. It won't. Nothing will come into your life except by the doorway of your thought, of your expectation, your faith. Concentration is indispensable to success in anything. As Dr. Julia Seaton says: "Concentration is the vital essence of all life, and without it there is no real purpose, no real control. Upon the power of concentration more than upon any other one thing, depends our law of attracting, controlling and mastering life's conditions."

If you feel discouraged because you are not getting on as you hoped you would, something is wrong. Your mind is not pulling in harmony with your effort on the physical plane. Something has arrested your progress, and that something is a mental stumbling-block which you yourself put in your path. You are not thinking yourself on, you are not putting yourself in the getting-on current by concentrating with confidence, with faith, along the line of your ambition. Discouragement, doubt, a wavering, divided mind, the scatteration of your efforts, something or other is neutralizing the force which would naturally take you to your goal. Perhaps you are frittering away your energies by giving your spare time to side-lines, trying to make a little success here, a little there, not giving the whole of yourself to your life work.

In Maine, the farmers say that it makes a horse a gawk to drive it without blinders, because its attention is drawn this way and that, which ruins the animal's gait and speed. Many a man has been ruined by not confining himself within sufficiently narrow limits to give concentration and direction to his energies.

Said Andrew Carnegie: "One great cause of failure of young men in business is lack of concentration. They are prone to seek outside investments, side-lines. The cause of many a surprising failure lies in so doing. Every dollar of capital and credit, every business thought, should be concentrated upon the one business upon which a man has embarked. He should never scatter his shot. *It is a poor business which will not yield better returns for increased capital than any outside investment.* No man or set of men or corporation can manage a business man's capital as well as he can manage it himself. The rule, 'Do not put all your eggs in one basket,' does not apply to a man's life-work."

Don't be afraid of being known as a man of one idea. The men who have moved the world have been men of this kind. It is the man who has his purpose burned into every fiber of his being, who has the faculty of focusing his scattered energies on one point as a burning glass focuses the scattered rays of the sun, that succeeds.

"When I have a subject in hand I study it profoundly," said Alexander Hamilton. "Day and night it is before me. My mind becomes pervaded with it. Then the success I make, the people are pleased to call genius. It is the fruit of thought and labor."

Concentration without genius will accomplish more than genius without concentration.

CHAPTER XVIII

"TIME IS MONEY"—AND MUCH MORE

Few of us realize the connection between the day, the **hour,** in which we are living, and our success, our happiness, **our** destiny.

It is so much easier to dream of a great big success to-morrow than to try to make to-day a big success.

When I see a young man who seizes every odd moment for self-improvement, who has an ambition to make each day count, then I know that there is something, a very big something, coming to him in the future.

Our to-days are the blocks with which we build our future. If these are defective, the whole structure of our life will correspond. That marvelous future which you have dreamed of so long will be exactly what you put into your to-days.

The world grants all opportunities to him who can use them. Power and fortune are hidden away in the hours and moments as they pass, awaiting the eye that can see, the ear that can hear, the hand that can do.

WHEN Queen Elizabeth of England was dying she said, "My kingdom for a moment!"

One of the richest men in the world said he would give millions of dollars to be assured of a few more years of life.

The late J. Pierpont Morgan used to say that every hour of his time was worth a thousand dollars. It was probably worth many thousands of dollars, even if measured by money alone, for the accumulation of a vast fortune was only an incident in Mr. Morgan's many-sided career.

But time is infinitely more valuable to us than is shown by its money-making power. I have never known of any person to make his life worth while in any direction until he came to the realization of the immense value of time. Time is our most precious asset, our greatest riches; because in it live our success, our happiness, our destiny.

Yet multitudes are engaged in killing time. Their chief aim in life is to fritter it away as rapidly as possible. They do not realize that this is infinitely more wasteful than it would be for a rich man to throw hundred dollar bills or valuable diamonds into the sea, or to do as Cleopatra did, dissolve priceless pearls in a glass of wine and drink them.

The future of a young man can be gauged to a nicety by the value he puts upon his time, especially his spare time. From the foundation of the American republic the greatest and most successful Americans have been men who not only in their youth but all through their lives made use of every spare moment in broadening their minds, adding to their knowledge, and developing their ability along their special line. The Washingtons, the Franklins, the Lincolns, the Burritts, the Morses, the Fields, the Edisons, the men in every line of endeavor all over the civilized world who have done great things for mankind and made themselves famous, achieved their great work not because they were geniuses, but because they got from every minute of time its full value.

"I have in my time known many famous in war, in statesmanship, in science, in the professions, and in business," said the late U. S. Senator Hoar of Massachusetts. "If I were asked to declare the secret of their success, I should attribute it, in general, not to any superiority of natural genius, but to the use they made in youth, after the ordinary day's work was over, of the hours which other men throw away or devote to idleness, or rest, or society. The great things in this world have been done by men of ordinary natural capacity, who have done their best. They have done their best by never wasting their time."

There are many so-called common or ordinary employees to-day, who, perhaps, think they haven't nearly as good a chance to rise as their more brilliant or showy companions, who will within a few years be filling high positions. The history of the past shows that every year brings out multitudes of giants from the ranks, often young fellows who are more surprised at their rapid advance than the employers who are watching them.

The only reason why anyone remains a common, ordinary employee, doing routine work and drawing a small salary, is not because he doesn't have the ability to rise higher, but because he is not awake to the possibilities in his spare time.

Charles M. Schwab had no more ability perhaps and no better chance to rise than the hundreds of other young men who were working with him at the Homestead plant of Andrew Carnegie when he started in at a dollar a day. The reason why he has become a millionaire and a king in his line is because he saw the necessity of a better education than he had had a chance to get up to that time, and devoted his evenings and spare time to making good his deficiencies, and particularly to acquiring special knowledge in regard to iron and steel. He was always on the alert to improve his opportunities, always preparing himself to be ready to fill positions next above him in case of a vacancy. That is why his rise was so rapid, why he is to-day one of the richest and most prominent business men in his line in the world, while his early fellow workers who preferred "a good time" to self-improvement in their spare time have never been heard from.

Speaking of those early days when he was beginning to attract attention at the Carnegie works, Mr. Schwab said:

"At that time science began to play an important part in the manufacture of steel. My salary at the age of twenty-one warranted me in marrying, so I had a home of my own. I believe in early marriages, as a rule. In my own house I rigged up a laboratory and studied chemistry in the evenings, determined that there should be nothing in the manufacture of steel that I would not know. Although I had received no technical education, I made myself master of chemistry, and of the laboratory, which proved of lasting value.

"The point I wish to make," continued he, "is that my experimental work was not in the line of my duty, but it gave me greater knowledge. Achievement is possible to a man who does something else besides his mere duty that attracts the attention of his superiors to him, as one who is equipping himself for advancement. An employer picks out his assistants from the best informed, most competent and conscientious."

"One is so tired after a day's work he does not feel like studying," is an excuse often urged by young people when reminded that they are not doing anything to advance themselves. It is only the excuse of those who are too lazy to work for what they want, or who lack the ambition to climb. It is well known that a change of occupation in the evening,— the bringing into play of a different set of muscles, brain tissues, ideas, and thoughts, generally rests rather than tires one. Of course every one should take a proper amount of time for needed recreation, exercise and rest, but very often those who claim they are too tired to study evenings waste more energy in foolish dissipation or dawdling aimlessly around doing nothing than they would spend in reading or study.

Only a short time ago I read of a young school teacher who learned six or seven languages in her spare time, and who managed, by earning some extra money evenings in teaching private pupils, to save enough money to go to Europe, to perfect herself in these languages. The enjoyment and breadth of culture she got out of her travels in the different European countries would have been a great reward for the sacrifices she made; but she got much more than that, for she advanced rapidly in her profession, and is now an instructor in French, German, and Italian in a high school for girls.

"The whole period of youth," says Ruskin, "is one essentially of formation, edification, instruction. There is not an hour of it but is trembling with destinies—not a moment of which, once passed, the appointed work can ever be done again, or the neglected blow struck on the cold iron." Millions of down-

and-outs are to-day bemoaning the loss of the golden opportunities they allowed to slip by in youth, the evenings and holidays they idled away when they might have been laying the foundations for a happy, successful future. But they couldn't eat their cake and have it too, and now they feel it is too late even to try to make good. They feel that they have nothing to look forward to but an old age of poverty and bitter regrets.

There is no magic which can give a youth a golden future when he is slipping careless, slipshod work and wasted hours into the fabric of to-day. Ambition, courage, industry, vim, energy, initiative, thoroughness poured into your day's work, and perseverance in self-improvement in your spare time, these are the ingredients warranted to make a golden future, to bring you wealth, knowledge, wisdom, power, fame—whatever you set your heart on.

"Believe me," said England's great statesman, William E. Gladstone, "when I tell you that thrift of time will repay you in after life with a usury of profit beyond your most sanguine dreams, and that waste of it will make you dwindle alike in intellectual and moral stature beyond your darkest reckoning." The way in which they spent their spare time has made all the difference between mediocrity and grand achievement to tens of thousands of men and women, who were intelligent enough in youth to know the value of the priceless odds and ends of time which others were recklessly wasting.

If some one offered to purchase a large percentage of your life power you would not think of selling it, even for a fabulous sum. It is what gives you your chance to make good, to make your life a masterpiece, and naturally you would not part with it. You would say that you could not afford to sell your birthright of power in which is wrapped up your whole destiny,—your enthusiasm, your zest, your career, your ambition. But do you realize that you are practically doing the same thing when you allow your most precious success asset, your time, to run away from you in all sorts of leaks; in sheer idleness, in dissipation, in superficial, silly pleasures, or worse, in pleasures which kill your self-respect and make you hate yourself the next day? If you would succeed in any adequate way, in a way at all

commensurate with your possibilities, you must
not only shut off all time leaks, but you must
also repair every leak in your mental and
physical system, and stop every output of energy that does not tell in rendering you more
fit to make your life the great success it is
possible for you to make it.

How often we are reminded of the value of
time by the expression, "Time is money." But
time is more than money; it is life itself; for
every separate moment as it flies takes with it
a part of our life span. Time is opportunity.
Time represents our success capital, our
achievement possibilities. Everything we hope
for, everything we dream of accomplishing, is
dependent on it.

"Short as life is," said Victor Hugo, "we
make it still shorter by the careless waste of
time." I would advise every youth starting
out in life to put that sentence up on the wall
in his sleeping room, and over his desk or work
bench, where it would constantly remind him
of the immense possibilities stored in the min-
utes and hours of every single day. If at the
outset of your career you resolve to make good
every day, and live up to your resolution, noth-

ing can keep you from being a successful man or woman, a superb character. You are the architect of your fate, the master of your destiny, and right now you are shaping your future. Every day is a step nearer to, or farther from, the goal of your ambition. The precious hours of youth are invaluable. The realization of all your dreams lives in them.

Letters come to me from time to time from young people deploring the fact that it is impossible for them to attend school or college. They say they have to work for a living, and therefore have no opportunity to acquire an education. They never stop to think that many of the most prominent men and women of the world have been self-educated. I do not mean that they have worked their way through school or college, but that they have actually gained an education in its widest and best sense, by their own efforts, with little or no actual schooling. You who complain that you have no opportunity to get an education, and therefore no opportunity to do anything worth while, read the lives of men and women who have lifted themselves into places of power by self-education, biographies like that of

Franklin, of Lincoln, of Greeley, of Garfield, of men of all nations who came from the direst poverty, and by sheer force of will and the wise use of every spare moment lifted themselves to the highest stations of life, to positions of honor, of great power and wealth.

As Hamilton W. Mabie said: "One of the prime qualities of a man of force and ability is his clear understanding of what can be done with the time and tools at his command. Such a man wastes no time in idle dreaming of the things he would do if he could go to college, or travel, or have command of long periods of uninterrupted time. He is not guilty of a feeble evasion of 'no possibility' for his career by getting behind adverse conditions. If the conditions are adverse, he gets in front of them, and so gets away from them.

"The question for each man to settle is not what he would do if he had means, time, influence, and educational opportunities; the question is what he will do with the things he has. The moment a young man ceases to dream or to bemoan his lack of opportunities and resolutely looks his conditions in the face, and resolves to change them, he lays the corner stone of a solid and honorable success."

No matter how limited your time, or how exacting your daily work, you can so train your mind, so cultivate yourself by reading and study in your spare moments, that you can, if you will, become an educated man or woman, with a much broader outlook on life and an infinitely greater earning capacity than the uneducated man or woman.

Andrew Carnegie, the young Scotch lad, for example, had only an elementary school education at the start, but by reading and studying in his leisure moments he acquired the culture that fruited in several books and many magazine articles on topics of worldwide interest, to say nothing of his business achievements and the immense fortune he acquired.

George Stephenson, inventor of the locomotive engine, seized every leisure moment as though it were gold. He educated himself and did much of his best work during his spare time. He learned to read and write at a night school, and studied arithmetic during the night shifts when he was assistant fireman in a colliery.

The lives and work of multitudes of the world's benefactors prove that no matter what investment a man may make in life, there is none so satisfactory as self-investment,—coining bits of leisure into knowledge and power.

The bigger the man the greater value he puts upon time. He regards it as a great asset, as the most precious capital which can enrich life. Whether his ambition be to acquire a fortune or to achieve success in some other direction, he knows that everything depends on what he does with his spare time. Weak natures, on the other hand, never regard time as a precious asset, they never want to pay the price which strong natures are willing to pay, to make their dreams come true. They can not resist the lure of pleasure for the sake of their ambition. They practice no more thrift in the use of their time than they do in the use of their money. They kill a lot of time without realizing that in doing this they are killing their prospects, killing their future, killing themselves.

"I will make this day worth while!" would

be a splendid daily motto for all of us to adopt. When you awake in the morning; when you start to work; and many times during the day, say to yourself: "I will make this day worth while. It shall not pass into the story of my life as time half wasted, or not utilized to the best advantage. No matter whether I feel like it or not, I am going to make this day count. I am going to make it stand out in my life as a red-letter day, one in which my work was effective, efficient." If you do this every day you will be surprised at the wonderful effect it will have upon your whole life. It will lift it to the highest point of your possible efficiency and effectiveness. It will mean everything to you both in character and financial returns.

Some one says: "All that time is lost which might be better employed." If all of us realized the truth of that, there would be more success and fewer failures in life. Each of us has the same number of hours in his day, the same number of days in his year, and the chief difference between the success and the failure lies in the use to which the hours and the days are put. Given the very same environment, the same chances to succeed, and one youth will rise to fame and fortune by the right use of the time that another recklessly wastes.

It is what we put into the passing moment, just that and nothing more, that makes up all of life, all of character, all of success. The harvest of our to-morrows will be like the seed we sow to-day. If we do not put that quality into the present moment which we expect in our success, in our character, in our life as a whole, it will not be there. If there is not energy, vim, courage, initiative, industry, a high quality of work in to-day the results of these cannot appear in your future. It is the daily ambition which starts out every morning with the firm resolution not to let the hours slip through one's fingers until one has wrung from them their utmost possibility that makes the successful day; and it is the accumulation of daily success s that makes the big life success, that enab'es the man to realize the ambitious dream of the boy.

CHAPTER XIX

THE POSITIVE VERSUS THE NEGATIVE MAN

The negative mind never gets anywhere; it can only destroy, tear down.

It is very easy to develop a negative state of mind, and it is very fatal to success. We must get rid of it before we can attract prosperity or develop efficiency.

We cannot act negatively without getting negative results.

The vacillating man, however strong in other respects, is always pushed aside in the race of life by the determined, positive, decisive man who knows what he wants to do, and does it. Even brains must give way to decision.

Even if sometimes wrong, it is better to decide positively and carry out your decision with energy than to be forever hanging in the balance, contemplating, and procrastinating.

Every important decision involves the letting go of something, and the more one tries to get away from the difficulty, the more he thinks over the thing to be decided, the more he entangles the whole situation.

It is not only necessary to keep your mind positive, but to be immune from all the enemies of prosperity and happiness, it must be vigorously positive.

It is the positive, vigorous mentality that does things, that makes things move. The negative character is always a weakling, a nobody, who follows in the beaten path.

IF WE could only learn always to talk and think decisively, constructively, what a wonderful civilization this would be! It is the strong, optimistic, expectant-of-good-things mind, the mind of faith, and of hope and confidence, belief in the good, that attracts the good. The mind of the pessimist attracts pessimistic products.

If you do not learn to decide firmly and finally and then act on your decision; if you waver and dilly-dally, allow yourself to be carried this way and that by conflicting circumstances, your life ship will always be adrift; you will never be anchored. You will always be at the mercy of storms and tempests, and will never make the port of prosperity.

When a young man asks my opinion of his chances for success in life, I try to find out something about his ability to decide things. If he can do this quickly, firmly, and finally, I am very sure he will win out. There is no other one quality which plays such an important part in business careers especially as the ability to decide things wisely, quickly, firmly, and finally.

The man who is made of winning material does not hesitate and dawdle and waver and balance on the fence. He jumps right in and tackles the hardest thing first, and goes through with it. Voltaire tells us that vacillation is the most prominent feature of weakness of character.

What we get out of life we do not get by physical force, but by the subtle power of mental attraction. We bring it to ourselves by making our minds magnets to attract it out of the great cosmic storehouse of intelligence. Out of the great ocean of supply that surrounds us we attract the things for which our mental attitude has an affinity. Some attract success, some failure; some attract opulence, plenty; others, poverty and lack. It all depends upon the difference in thought whether it is positive or negative, constructive or destructive. Negative thoughts demagnetize the mind so that it attracts just the opposite of what we want.

People who plod along in mediocrity, or who fail in life, might make a very creditable life record if they could only keep the things out of their minds which make them negative. It is their discouraging moods and all of their enemy thoughts,—their doubts, fears, worries, uncertainties, and their lack of confidence in themselves that kill the creative power of the mind and make it negative.

The negative mind never gets anywhere. It is the positive mind that radiates force and pushes its way in the world. A negative mind can only destroy, tear down.

Many people dwell so much upon their failure to get on in the world, their poverty, their misfortunes, that they develop a real failure atmosphere; they surround themselves with destructive, tearing-down thoughts, disintegrating suggestions, until they make impossible that mental condition, that positive mental attitude which creates, produces.

We are just beginning to learn that we can not only control our moods and all of our thoughts, but that we can also control our environment, because our environment is largely our objectified thought, feeling, emotion, and mental attitude. We make our own world by our thoughts, our motives.

As long as you keep your mind positive and creative you will have courage, initiative, and sound judgment, you will be a producer. But the moment you become discouraged and blue, your ability, your mind, becomes demagnetized, negative, and you are no longer a creator or a producer. Your decision wobbles, your judgment is weak and uncertain, your whole mental kingdom is demoralized. Keep your mind positive by refusing to admit to it such traitors as doubt, discouragement, fear or worry. They are your fatal enemies. You can never succeed while you entertain them. Drive them out. Don't leave the doors of your mind open to them.

Be known as a man of great faith regarding everything in the world; believe that everything is right in the world because God made it, God ordered it. Believe only in the best. Live success; walk about among your fellows as though you were successful, with a triumphant, victorious air; show that you are victory organized. Never fear failure; don't visualize it; don't picture poverty or have a horror of it, for this tends to make it a reality and keeps away from you the very things you desire.

"What is the use of dreaming about the wonderful things I am going to do in the future? There is no such achievement in store for me. I am not a genius. I must content myself with an ordinary career." These negative thoughts and assertions permeate the atmosphere of most homes and chill the youthful ardor of the children with the result that their ambition sags, their ideals shrivel, and, having no great life incentive, they drop into a humdrum routine and fall far below the level they might have attained.

It is criminal not to correct the tendency to negativeness in a child's mind. It is not very difficult to cultivate a positive habit of thinking and acting if undertaken when a child is young. With the adult it is not so easy, but it is possible.

When you long for something that it is perfectly legitimate for you to have, sow your affirmation seed in perfect confidence that it will bloom in reality. Say to yourself, "God is no respecter of persons. He is not partial in his treatment of His children. They all have the same rights, the same privileges. He will give me through my own effort what I need, what I ask for. The poorest, most ragged wretch that crawls has just as many hours in his day as has the richest and most powerful magnate. I can and I will do what

I long to do. I will be what I desire to be."

Whatever you do, don't set up in your mind and in that of others, a picture of yourself as a weak, ineffective, negative personality.

If you are constantly depreciating yourself, other people will think there is a reason for it, that you are not worthy, that there is something about you that they do not know about as a basis of your own judgment. Why should not others think meanly of you if you do yourself?

If you carry about with you a negative mental attitude yours will be a negative life. You cannot act negatively without getting negative results.

Negative people do not start vigorous, positive vibrations; they are so passive and so susceptible to the influences about them that their negative minds take off all of the negative vibrations from all the cross currents from other negative minds.

It is perfectly possible to make our mentality so vigorously positive that, no matter what conflicting currents or vibrations from other negative, discordant minds strike us, they find no response. Then we are immune to all negativeness; we can walk through all sorts of adverse conditions about us without responding, because we do not vibrate to the negative thought and the negative condition, and we can still keep our robust, positive poise.

Living in the stronger thought makes us stronger. People with a vigorous, positive mental attitude, people with a strong, firm decision, people with great faith, have a much stronger mentality than do negative minds, because they habitually live in a more vigorous mental attitude, and a positive mental attitude makes for growth, for mental enlargement. We all know the negative man, the man who never has any opinion of his own, who is always asking other people's advice and depending upon others. The negative character is always a weakling. The negative man in any community is the nobody. It is the positive, vigorous mentality that does things, that makes things move, that puts things through. It is the positive man who does his own thinking; who dares to step out of the beaten path and blaze his own way; who dares to have opinions of his own and dares to express them. This is the sort of man who gains the respect and confidence of mankind.

A lot of people go through life doing little things, because their negative thought paralyzes their initiative; they do not dare undertake anything important. The negative mind, the man who is afraid to act, who is always deliberating or hesitating, never accomplishes much.

The leader is always characterized by positive qualities. He rules by his vigorous affirmatives. There is nothing negative or minus about him. The positive man, the natural leader, is always assertive, while the negative man shrinks, effaces himself, waits for some-one else to take the initiative.

One of the most pathetic sights in the world is the man who never has any opinion of his own,—the backboneless, shiftless, slovenly, negative man, who never differs from you, whose only opinion is assent to the one you express. We instinctively despise such a weakling, a man who never opposes us, who always says "yes, yes," to everything we say.

We want leaders and originators more than we want followers or imitators. We have enough, and to spare, of those who are willing to lean on others. We want our young people to depend on themselves. We want them to be so educated and trained that their qualities of leadership, their originality and their individuality, will be emphasized and strengthened instead of obliterated.

All negative thinking, all negative mental attitudes, such as doubting one's ability, hesitating to undertake things, the habit of putting off, waiting for more favorable conditions, and of reconsidering one's decisions, are deadly enemies of initiative. If one does not cultivate a positive mental attitude he will have a weak, wishy-washy initiative, and initiative is the executive officer of the other faculties. It is the brain leader.

Do not forget that the force that is going to project you to the success and prosperity goal is actually inside of you. Do not look to others to push you, to give you a pull or to use their influence. Your resources, your assets, are right inside of you; they are nowhere else.

If you feel paralyzed by the very responsibility of deciding things, beginning things of your own accord, make up your mind that if you ever are to amount to anything in the world you must strangle this habit. The only way to do this is to form the counter-habit of starting out every morning with the grim resolution not to allow yourself, during the day, to waver, to wait for somebody to show you the way. Resolve that during the entire day you are going to be a pusher, a leader; that you are not going to be a trailer, not going to wait for somebody to tell you what to do and how to do it; that you are going to take the initiative, start things yourself, put them through without advice. Determine to carry a positive mental attitude. This will sharpen the faculties, put a keen edge upon them, and make the mind alert and eager for opportunities.

It is not only necessary to keep your mind positive, but to be immune from all the enemies of your success and happiness it must be vigorously positive. When the mind is saturated with all sorts of negation, with the thoughts of sickness, of failure and poverty, it becomes chronically discordant, and gradually deteriorates. Form the habit of talking up, not down, of talking optimism instead of pessimism. Cut criticism, fault-finding and blame out of your vocabulary. One of the first signs of deterioration in many minds is a tendency to negativeness; to hold the discordant, belligerent, envious, jealous mental attitude. This is just as abnormal as is chronic melancholy, gloom, and despondency. These indicate an abnormal or diseased condition of the mind. Try to see things from a large, generous standpoint; hold a large consciousness. Show everybody that you have a great faith in humanity, in your calling, and in yourself. Resolve to keep the negatives out of your life. You are too large for jealousy or envy, too big for worry, or to be anxious about your career, or about your future.

Making yourself positive to everybody and everything you contact with in life is what counts. This is the key to mastership, to success and prosperity.

CHAPTER XX

THRIFT AND PROSPERITY

If you would be sure that you are beginning right, begin to save. The habit of saving money, while it stiffens the will, also brightens the energies.   THEODORE ROOSEVELT.

Enter into a compact with yourself to save a certain amount every week out of your salary.

The little difference between what we earn and what we spend is capital.

Thrift is the friend of man, a civilization builder.

The practice of thrift gives an upward tendency to the life of the individual, and to the life of the nation; it sustains and preserves the highest welfare of the race.

Nothing makes a business man so absolutely independent as ready cash.

It is the "man with the savings-bank habit who seldom gets laid off; he's the one who can get along without you, but you cannot get along without him."

Thrift means wise management of what you have—money, time, energies, opportunities.

BENJAMIN FRANKLIN is one of the most inspiring examples of what the practice of thrift can do for the poorest boy or girl in this land of opportunities. Son of a poor tallow chandler and soap boiler, the fifteenth child in a family of seventeen, he began at the age of ten to earn his living by working in his father's shop. From these humble beginnings he succeeded, entirely by his own efforts, in becoming one of the world's greatest men—a distinguished patriot, scientist, statesman, inventor, diplomat, philosopher, author, and, last but not least, a noted humorist.

All this he accomplished by the practice of thrift. That does not mean merely economy in financial matters, the wisest expenditure of his income, but the wisest expenditure of his time and efforts in all the business of life. For to him thrift meant not only prudence in business and money spending, but the conservation of health, of energy, of life capital, and the utmost development of all his natural resources. As well as being the most thrifty, Franklin was the most generous of men, and would share his last cent with one who needed it.

One of Franklin's favorite maxims—one that he literally lived by himself—was "God helps those who help themselves." And the first lesson for those who would help themselves to learn is the one that he constantly taught—Thrift.

Headed with a picture of Benjamin Franklin, the great apostle of thrift, a calendar, issued by the Y. M. C. A. in New York, has this slogan—"Make Your Money Mean More." Then, it gives the "Ten Commandments for a Young Man's Financial Life."

1.—Work and Earn.
2.—Make a Budget.
3.—Record Your Expenditures.
4.—Have a Bank Account.
5.—Carry Life Insurance.
6.—Own Your Own Home.
7.—Make a Will.
8.—Pay Your Bills Promptly.
9.—Invest in Reliable Securities.
10.—Share With Others.

If you "forge these links of success into your character," as the calendar suggests, you will not only develop a self-reliant, vigorous type of manhood or womanhood, but you will also be laying the foundation of enduring prosperity, contentment, and happiness.

Every man knows that it is easier to earn

money than to save it; so if there is any one link in the "Ten Commandments" the wage earner, the man or woman of limited means, should pay special attention to, it is the second, "Make a Budget." And here again the Y.M. C.A. is meeting a great need in supplying "A Budget Book With a Conscience," which shows the best way to plan the expenditure of your income, and how to keep an accurate account of your income and outlay.

From Benjamin Franklin to Sir Thomas Lipton, thousands of successful men in every field have given testimony to the value of thrift, or economy, as a wealth and happiness maker. Lipton says it is "the first great principle of all success. It creates independence, it gives a young man standing, fills him with vigor, it stimulates him with the proper energy; in fact, it brings to him the best part of any success— happiness and contentment."

Unless you make it a cast-iron rule to lay aside a certain percentage of your earnings each week, each month, you will never succeed in becoming a really independent man or woman. You will always be at the mercy of circumstances. No matter how small it may

be, or if you have to go without a great many
things you think you need, put a portion of
your earnings away every year where it will
be absolutely safe. You don't know what this
will mean to you in case of illness, accident, or
some unlooked for emergency when a little
ready money may save you great suffering or
financial ruin.

The wise expenditure of one's income, however small it may be, involves the same principles as the investment and handling of the
business man's capital. And the successful
business man carries these principles into the
conduct of all his affairs, his personal and
household expenditures as well as those relat-
ing directly to his business. Even multi-mil-
lionaires have to be thrifty or their millions
would take wings.

In his little book "Succeeding With What
You Have," Charles M. Schwab says: "Not
long ago the expenses of running my New
York home got exorbitant. I called in the
steward and said to him: 'George, I want to
strike a bargain with you. I will give you
ten per cent of the first thousand dollars you
save in house expenses, twenty-five per cent

of the second thousand, and one-half of the third thousand.' The expense of operating the house was cut in two."

I once sent an interviewer to Marshall Field to ask him, among other things, what he considered the turning-point in his career, and his answer was: "Saving the first five thousand dollars I ever had, when I might just as well have spent the modest salary I made. Possession of that sum, once I had it, gave me the ability to meet opportunities. That I consider the turning-point." John Jacob Astor, the founder of the Astor fortune, said that if it had not been for the saving of his first thousand he might have died in the almshouse.

What a pathetic thing it is to see, as we do on every hand, well-educated, well-bred men and women, people with a great deal of ability, but with no money sense, going about with practically nothing ahead of them, between themselves and want, spending everything as they go! What a pathetic story the charity organizations could tell about people who have been in better circumstances, but who have lost their money, of people who have never

been able to lay up anything, to put by anything, for a "rainy day."

What an assurance and sense of protection
we get from the consciousness of a little "nest-
egg," a little money laid up for the future,
something to stand between us and possible
emergency or want, no matter what might
happen to us.

No one can feel easy or safe who is living
from hand to mouth. How many poor people
in our great cities are constantly dispossessed,
put out on the sidewalk, oftentimes when a
parent or some other member of the family is
ill, because they can't pay the rent, and this is
often due to the lack of early training in thrift
and wise economy; no provision made for an
emergency; nothing laid up for a rainy day.

I have no sympathy for the rainy-day philosophy of many people; the rainy-day fear and
terror, that cheeseparing saving, pinching,
stingy policy. Such people make the very
rainy day they are trying to guard against.
It is the good sense, the wise precaution, which
gives a reasonable provision for future needs,
or for accidents, or for emergency, or for anything which may impair one's earning capacity,

or any loss which may result from fire or flood, that wins our approval.

The saving habit, the bank-book habit, is an indication of the ambition to get on and up in the world. It is also an indication of many other good success qualities. The bank-book habit is seldom found in bad company.

The habit of thrift not only opens the door to opportunity, but is a safeguard against our own weaknesses, our gullibility, the tendency to scatter our earnings and make fools of ourselves. The saving of money so often means the saving of a man. It means cutting out indulgences or avoiding vicious habits. It often means health in the place of dissipation. It means a clear instead of a cloudy and muddy brain. It means that a man has vision, foresight, intelligence in planning and providing for his future. In fact, the thrift habit, the habit of saving, is not only one of the foundation-stones of a fortune, but also of character.

Theodore Roosevelt once wisely said, "If you would be sure that you are beginning right, begin to save. The habit of saving money, while it stiffens the will also brightens the energies."

The moment a young man begins to put aside money, systematically, and to make wise investments, he becomes a larger man. He begins to have a broader view of life. He begins to have more confidence in himself, in his ability, in his power to shoulder responsibility, to make his own program, to be his own boss. In early learning the lesson of thrift, he has taken the first step in the development of a sturdy character, the sort of character that distinguishes the best type of self-made man —the Benjamin Franklins of the race.

Nothing will do more to help a young man to get credit and gain for him the assistance of successful people than the reputation for thrift, of having the saving habit,—of having something ahead, something laid by, whether in government bonds, or in a life insurance policy, or in some other investment. Such thrift gives him standing.

A prominent business man says: "Give me the youth who saves to make the man worth while."

If you want to make your dreams of a prosperous future come true you will enter into a compact with yourself to save a certain amount every week out of your salary. No matter how small this may be, or if you have to go without a great many things that you think you need; put this certain percentage of your earnings where it will be absolutely safe. This may mean riches to you in the future. A little ready money attracts opportunities. I have known of young men to get a splendid opportunity to start in business for themselves on five hundred dollars, some on less. Many a fortune has been started on less than a thousand dollars. The head of five big stores in New York told me he began business with three hundred dollars. Frank Woolworth, who built up the mammoth five and ten cent store business, started with something like three hundred dollars of his own, borrowing enough to bring it up to five hundred. Several of his first stores were failures, but he was not a failure. He had an idea and his small earnings helped him to back up his idea and to make his dreams come true.

The power of money is usually not half appreciated by young men and young women. This is a land of opportunity, and good chances

are constantly coming to those who have the
ready cash. How often we hear people plead
as an excuse for not seizing a rare opportunity
for investment, that they hadn't the money!
Multitudes of men have been obliged to let
splendid opportunities pass because of this
same lack. Great bargains for cash everywhere have been offered and only comparatively few men have had the reserve funds or
the ready cash to avail themselves of these
splendid chances.

Some of the shrewdest business men I know
tell me that there is nothing that pays the
business man so well, in the long run, as to
keep money in the bank, ready for an emergency, ready for an unexpected opportunity or
a great bargain. It gives one a great sense of
security to know that he is prepared for any
ordinary emergency, that he has ready cash to
help him. We can never tell when illness or
accident may impair our earning capacity, or
when some unforeseen emergency may make an
unexpected call upon us. The thrifty man is
never caught unprepared.

There are opportunities to save all around

us. The facilities for saving are unparalleled and the rewards are certain.

When we get a little money ahead it arouses enthusiasm to add to it. It is a perpetual suggestion, when we are tempted to spend, that we try to save. It is a little easier to say "No" when inclined to spend foolishly or for things which are really not worth while. Our savings are a constant encouragement, a tonic, a stimulant. His small savings have kept many a young man from falling into temptations which might have crippled or ruined him.

The little difference between what we earn and what we spend is capital. A little ready money suggests to young people just establishing a home wonderful possibilities in the way of comforts, the means of self-culture and growth. It means a little better reading matter, better books and periodicals. It means a possible college course later on for the children, and old age protection. It means less worry and less anxiety about the future, exemption from the fear of coming to want, or that those dear to us may suffer. It may mean a good physician, a skillful surgeon, instead of a bungler when sickness enters our home.

"I have been asked," says a great business man, "to define the true secret of success. It is thrift in all its phases, and especially, thrift as applied to savings. Saving is the first great principle of success. It creates independence, it gives a young man standing, fills him with vigor, it stimulates him with the proper energy; in fact, it brings to him the best part of any success—happiness and contentment."

Can you desire anything better in your future than these?

I AM—?

I am stored-up happiness.

I lead the way to peace, power, and plenty. I bring you freedom from anxiety and worry over the living problem.

I am a friend alike of the rich and the poor.

I am common sense applied to life in all sorts of ways.

I am a tower of strength in youth and a staff in old age.

I increase hope, confidence, assurance, certainty as to the future.

I was one of the chief factors in the winning of the World War.

I am the best form of insurance against poverty and failure. I remove the shadow of the poorhouse.

I make for health, for efficiency, for the highest possible welfare of the individual.

I kill that "rainy day" dread; in fact, I do away with the "rainy day" altogether.

I put hope into the heart of man, a light into human eyes that was never there before.

I put people in a position to take advantage of all sorts of opportunities for investment, for advancement, to take advantage of chances that, but for me, would be lost.

I mean the best physicians, the most skilled surgeons, the best hospitals in case of need, as well as the best health resorts.

I make possible a needed vacation, rest, recreation and travel. I mean leisure, more living with natural art and with the beautiful things in the world.

I mean better opportunities for your children, better schools, better clothing, a more refining environment, greater security for their future.

I show you how to make the most of your income; how to expend the margin to the best advantage; how to make the wisest investments of your time, your strength and your ability as well as your money.

I am the friend of man, a civilization builder. I not only give an upward tendency to the life of the individual, but also to the life of a nation. I sustain and preserve the highest welfare of the race.

I safeguard the future; I enable you to work with confidence, to look up and not down, to rise superior to your surroundings.

I keep thousands of people out of the penitentiary; prevent them from committing theft and other crimes.

I increase the confidence of others in struggling young men and add tremendously to their credit.

I am an employee's best recommendation, for I belong to a large and most excellent family. Every employer knows that the employee who cultivates me has many other sterling qualities, such as honesty, thoroughness, ambition, reliability, foresight, prudence.

I am a symbol of character, of stability, of

self-control; a proof that a man is not a victim of his appetites and weaknesses, but their master.

I am often the saviour of a man, cutting off indulgences and vicious habits, putting health in the place of dissipation and insuring a clear brain instead of a cloudy, befuddled one.

I am the enemy of that great curse of mankind—debt—which wrecks multitudes of homes, causes divorce, blasts love, and destroys all peace of mind.

I am that which helps a man to lift his head above the crowd; to be independent, self-reliant, and to stand for something in the world.

Multitudes of families are homeless, moneyless, and are enduring all sorts of hardship, privation, and humiliation because the husbands and fathers never took me into partnership.

The failure army, to-day, is largely recruited by people who never learned to know me, who ridiculed the suggestion of needing me, who rather despised and looked down on me as standing for meanness and penuriousness and as being an enemy of their enjoyment.

I am the best friend of woman. I make her a better business woman, a better housekeeper, a better wife and mother, a better citizen. I help her to make herself independent, self-reliant, and teach her how to finance herself.

However you make your living, whether by the work of your hand or of your brain, in a trade or in a profession, at home or in the shop, whether your income be small or large, you will always be placed at a disadvantage, will always be taking chances with your future security and happiness, unless you have me as a working partner.

I am an incentive to high living, the simple life and high thinking. I urge spending upward, living upward, dwelling in honesty, in simplicity, living the life that is worth while, the genuine life, the life that will give enduring satisfaction.

I am the beginning of real success; that which puts a foundation under your air castles, that which makes your dreams come true, which builds that "home of my own" to which every healthy, ambitious young person looks forward as the culmination of his hopes.

I AM THRIFT

CHAPTER XXI

AS A MAN EXPECTETH SO IS HE

We never can get more out of ourselves than we expect. If we expect large things, if we hold the large mental attitude toward our work, toward our life, we shall get much greater results than if we depreciate ourselves, and only look for little things.

The habit of expecting great things of ourselves calls out the best that is in us.

No one can become prosperous while he really expects, or half expects, to remain poor. We tend to get what we expect, and to expect little is to get little.

We ask little things, we expect little things, and thus we limit our supply.

There is a tremendous power in the habit of anticipating good things, of believing that we shall realize our ambition; that our dreams will come true. Multitudes queer their success at the very outset by anticipating bad things, expecting that they are going to fail, that their dreams will never be realized.

WHEN I was graduated from a New Hampshire academy my greatest stimulus to further endeavor was my favorite teacher's belief in me. Taking me by the hand at parting, as he bade me good-bye, he said: "My boy, I expect to hear from you,—that the world will hear from you,—in the future. Don't disappoint me. I believe in you, and can see something in you that you do not see in yourself."

There is only one thing more stimulating, more helpful, in the struggle for success, than the knowledge that others—our teachers, our parents, our friends and relatives—believe in us and expect great things of us; that is, to expect great things of ourselves. The difference between what two people get out of life, what they accomplish, and what they represent to others, depends upon the difference in what they expect of themselves.

A general who goes into a battle expecting to be beaten will be beaten. His expectation of defeat communicates itself to his army, demoralizes it at the start, and makes it impossible for the men to do their best. It is the same in the battle of life. To enter it with the expectation of defeat, is to be defeated before you begin. If you desire to succeed you must show your confident expectancy of success in your very presence. You must also live day by day in the very soul of expectancy of splendid things which are coming to you.

Working for one thing and expecting the opposite can bring only one result—failure. Every time you say you don't expect ever to be anything, or to get anything, or to accomplish anything worth while, you are neutralizing the efforts you are making to be or to get or to do what you want. Our expectations must correspond with our endeavor. If we are convinced that we are never going to be really happy, that we are destined to plod along in discontent and wretchedness, to suffer all our lives, we shall tend to get what we expect. To be ambitious for happiness and yet always expect to be miserable, to continually doubt our ability to get what we long for, whatever it may be, is like getting on a train which is headed east when we wish to go west. We must *expect* to go in the direction of our desire, of our longing and effort. If you would succeed in what you are trying to do or to be, you must turn your back upon failure, blot out of your mind every thought, every picture, every suggestion of failure, and head toward success.

When, through a series of reverses and disappointments, a man has lost his grip upon himself, and feels convinced that he cannot possibly get on his feet; when he expects nothing but failure, there is only one thing you can do for him,—try to arouse his hope; to restore his lost faith; to show him that, being divine, there is something in him which can never fail; that he and his Maker are one, and that, working together, they are a majority in any situation.

I have just received some manuscripts accompanied by a letter, in which the writer says: "I know the enclosed are nothing like your articles, for I couldn't write like you no matter how hard I might try. I don't expect you will want to publish these, but thought I would send them along because of the possibility that you might."

Now, at the very outset, this writer prejudiced me against his articles by his self-expressed inferiority and the suggestion that they were not worth publishing, and would probably be returned. It was as though a young man should start out in a disheartened mood to look for a job, discouragement in his face and in his every action, and should say to a prospective employer: "I don't think you will hire me; I didn't expect any luck when I came in, but thought I would try. I haven't much confidence in myself, and don't know that I can do work along this line. I doubt very much if I should suit you. Still I will try my best if you want to give me a chance, though I don't believe you will, for I never have any luck in hunting jobs."

This may sound ridiculous, but it expresses the mental attitude which multitudes of people hold toward the thing they long for and are striving to attain. They never expect to succeed in anything they undertake; never expect to be comfortable, to say nothing of having the luxuries and refinements of life. They expect only failure and poverty, and do not understand that this very expectancy increases the power of their mental magnet to attract these things, even though they are trying to get away from them.

I was recently talking with a man who is a good illustration of what this mental attitude does for us. He told me that for many years he had been working very hard, with no vacations, no let up in his efforts; that he worked holidays and most of his Sundays, and yet had never gotten anywhere and never expected to; that, in fact, things seemed to be in a conspiracy to disappoint and defeat him. "Of course you haven't succeeded, my friend, because you never expected to," I said to myself. "Moreover, you never gave yourself a chance. Holding your nose to the grindstone all this time, fearing and expecting poverty, failure, disappointment, limitation, defeat in everything, has made you a magnet for these things and drawn you into a failure rut."

We don't necessarily get what we work for; it is what we expect that comes to us. What you fear, as well as what you long for, is headed your way. All your fears, all your doubts, all your failure thoughts are taking shape in your life, molding conditions to their likeness; and no matter how hard you work for the thing you want, if you hold constantly in mind negative, discouraged thoughts; if you expect failure instead of success, evil instead of good, it is what you expect that will come to you. In other words, your thought is

the creative force that molds and determines
the conditions of your life.

"You must have birds in your heart,
Madam, before you can find them in the
bushes," said John Burroughs, the great natu-
ralist, to a woman who complained that no
birds ever came to her orchard, while he counted
a score or more there, even while she uttered
her plaint. It is what you hold in your heart,
what you believe will manifest itself to you,
that comes into your life. No one can accomplish anything great in this world who is confident that he was made to do little things,
and is satisfied with an inferior position, hopeless of being anything but an underling all
his life. On the other hand, a man who expects great things of himself is constantly trying to open a little wider the doors of his narrow life, to extend his limited knowledge, to
reach a little higher, to get a little farther on
than those around him. He has enough of
the divine disposition to spur him on to nobler
endeavors; he has a quenchless ambition to
make the most of himself.

No matter what the conditions of your birth,
it is you who shape your career, fashion your

life for happiness or unhappiness, success or failure. It is true of all men and women that—

"They themselves are makers of themselves."

If you want to live the larger life, the happy, useful life, you must think the larger life; you must enlarge your model of yourself and of your possibilities; you must expect to realize your ideal of yourself and of the thing you long to do; for, as a man expecteth, so will his happiness, so will his life be.

It doesn't matter what we are trying to do, it is the hope and expectancy of success that nerves us to put forth our greatest effort; arms us with the assurance that compels success. The greatest difference, for instance, between the A1 salesman and the mediocre one is the difference in their mental attitude.

"Beaten before he began"; "Didn't believe he was going to get the order," is written all over some salesmen. In trying to get orders they lack the hope, the expectation of success, the assurance and self-confidence that presage victory. They don't know the psychology of salesmanship; that it consists in holding the conviction of success always in mind, and so they fall down before the slightest opposition.

There are thousands of second-rate salesmen who have enough ability to make crackerjacks, but who fail to get results because of their doubts and fears. At every little objection made by a prospect, they keep thinking and saying to themselves: "There, I am going to lose that man; I just feel it in my bones. I wish I could get an order from him, but it's no use; he's not going to sign." They do not realize that they are communicating their own doubts and fears to their prospect. It doesn't take a very sensitively organized person to feel the negative, failure atmosphere, and when he first lays his eyes upon one of those timid, doubting salesmen, the prospect knows that he is not a winner. Instead of victory, he sees defeat in his face; and if defeat is in a man's face he can't win no matter how much ability he has. His failure atmosphere repels everyone he contacts with.

Negative minds never make great salesmen or great anything else, because they don't build; they tear down. They are not creative, but destructive. They go through life closing the very doors ahead of them which they long to open; pulling with one hand, so to speak, on the door-knob, while at the same time holding a foot of doubt against that very door which they are trying to open. If they affirm their belief that there are good things for them, almost before they leave their lips they neutralize their affirmations by their secret doubts. They say one thing, but expect the opposite, just like the woman who prayed to the Lord to remove the sand heap from her yard, and when she got through praying looked out and said, "There it is, just as I expected! Of course the Lord didn't remove it!" That is the trouble with most of us. We pray and we work hard for things, and when we don't get them it is, "just as we expected." We couldn't get what we wanted and longed for because there was no faith, no belief, back of our efforts and our prayers. You know what St. James says of the man who doubts and fears and has no faith: "Let not that man think that he shall receive anything of the Lord."

Some people cannot understand how it is that bad men, cruel, brutal, conscienceless men, often succeed so well in their business. They succeed by the exercise of the mental law that like thoughts produce like results. This law works as unerringly as any physical law. It is neither ethical nor unethical. It is scientific. It is an inexorable principle, a changeless fact, that what we hold persistently in the mind is ultimately objectified in the body, in the life, whether it relates to our health, to our success or to our happiness. Ignorance of the law does not save us from the consequences of its violation, just as ignorance of our state or federal laws does not condone an offense against them.

This is why it is so important that children should be trained in right thinking from the start. Every child should be reared to expect big things of himself: to understand that the Creator sent him here on an important mission, and that he must prepare himself for a life of achievement. Being a child of Omnipotence, of the All-Supply, man is the heir of all that is; health, success and happiness are his divine birthright, and every child should grow up with the conviction that good things instead of evil are waiting for him; that the longings of his heart, the yearnings of his soul, are prophecies of what he may become if he does his part in making a thorough preparation for his life work.

Do you realize that your environment to-day, your achievement, and your poverty or prosperity are really made up of your expectations of the past; what you expected of yourself years ago, when you started out in life? If you have been true to your vision of a successful future, and have backed up your faith, your ability, with hard work and intelligent endeavor, you have worked in harmony with the law and are reaping the harvest of your thought and endeavor. If, on the other hand, you find yourself poverty - stricken and wretched, you have violated the law, and your only hope of bettering your condition is to turn about face and go the other way. Work with the law, not against it. Work for what you want, but work with confidence, with the hope, the belief, that you will get it.

Expecting to be happy; expecting to be successful; expecting to win out in our undertakings; expecting health instead of disease; expecting good luck instead of ill-luck; expecting harmony instead of discord and trouble; expecting to make friends wherever we go; expecting to be thought well of, to stand for something in our community,—this is to establish relations with the things we want and are working for; it is to attract them to us: for as a man expecteth so is he; so has he.

CHAPTER XXII

"I CAN'T AFFORD IT"—THE HABIT OF GOING WITHOUT

People who are always fearing the future, who always see rocks, shoals, and all sorts of snags and dangers ahead, who are forever preparing for a "rainy day," not only attract the very things they fear, but also lose all the joy and happiness of living.

You will never be anything but a beggar while you think beggarly thoughts, but a poor man while you think poverty, a failure while you think failure thoughts.

Train yourself persistently away from the thought of limitation, away from the thought of lack, of want, of pinched supply. Thinking abundance, and defying limitation, will open up your mind and set your thought currents toward a greatly increased supply.

When we learn the art of seeing opulently, instead of stingily; when we learn to think without limits, how not to cramp ourselves by our limiting thought, we shall find that the thing we are seeking is seeking us, and that to-morrow it will meet us half way.

You do not inherit poverty, squalor, humiliating limitations. Lack and want have nothing whatever to do with God's children. Your inheritance is rich, sublime beyond description.

Do you know that every time you say "I can't afford it, such things are for others, but not for me," or, "I have been poor and had to

300

deny myself things all my life, and I expect it will always be so," you are closing the doors to prosperity?

If you want to realize prosperity and plenty you must dismiss forever from your mind the can't-afford-it thought, the thought that you can't afford anything which is good for you, anything which will contribute to the growth or highest possible development of the man or woman. It is your birthright to have these things. They belong to you by divine heritage, and you should claim them. The Creator intended that His children should have plenty, and the best of everything that is good for them, that will contribute to growth, enlargement of character, and happiness.

The idea that riches are possible only to those who have superior advantages, more ability, or those who have been favored by fate, is false and demoralizing. The Creator has given man dominion over a world teeming with riches for all, not for a favored few. If we claim our inheritance and *work in harmony with His laws* we will have the abundance and happiness He meant we should have. We will be glorious successes. It is not in our nature that we are paupers, but in our mean, stingy estimate of ourselves and our powers.

To me, one of the most pitiable things in the world is a family where the parents, through mistaken ideas of economy, fail to bring up their children generously, who refuse to furnish them with the mental food, the change, the variety, the amusement, that are so necessary to their largest possible development.

How many parents, fearing future want, hoard their money and starve their children's minds, stunt their growth, so that they become dwarfed human beings instead of the superb personalities they might have been if the parents had made a generous effort in their education, in the development of their mental growth!

People are often obliged to go through life exhibiting deplorable ignorance, and are many times blamed for this when their parents were really at fault. They never gave them as children the nourishment, the mental food necessary to develop their larger qualities, their greater possibilities. They are compelled to plod along in mediocrity, so far as mentality and personality are concerned, because they never have had a fair chance. Their ability, their brains, were never backed up with the proper preparation for the larger possible life.

Many of these parents, perhaps most of them, fully intended to be generous to their children, but the habit of saving, the fear of coming to want, which in time develops into a strangling, dwarfing, blighting greed, kept them putting off from year to year a present privilege and duty. They did not put the emphasis on the right thing, to the lifelong detriment of those they loved more than anything else in the world.

True economy is not parsimony, miserliness. It is neither extravagance nor meanness. It means a wise expenditure, an expenditure which brings the largest results. It is being good to ourselves in as large and scientific a way as possible. It means that we should always have the best we can possibly afford when the thing has any reference to our physical and mental health, to our growth in efficiency and power. It often means very liberal spending. It is a perpetual protest against putting the emphasis on the wrong thing.

"Extravagance leads to insubordination and parsimony to meanness," we are told.

Don't deceive yourself by going through life patronizing cheap things, wearing cheap clothes, looking seedy, with the belief that you are doing the wisest thing. Remember that your appearance will largely determine your status in society. The world accepts or rejects us by the evidence of our personality, the impression we make. The feeling that you can't afford this and you can't afford that; always dwelling upon something cheap, cheapens your life, cheapens your mentality, limits and narrows it, dwarfs your personality and makes anything but a favorable impression. Wise, thrifty, and often generous expenditure in the thing which helps us along the line of our ambition, which will make a good impression, secure us quick recognition, and help our promotion, is often an infinitely better investment than putting money in a savings-bank.

The secret of health, of success and happiness, is largely in being good to one's self, in putting one's self in a superb condition, so that one is always able to do the biggest thing possible to him, always ready to take advantage of whatever opportunities come his way. Anything which prevents a person from attaining this high-water mark of efficiency is a sin against true economy. Every young man should have an understanding with himself at the outset that he will have nothing to do with the false economy that results in lowered vitality or efficiency, that anything which tends to cut down his power, even by a small fraction, is poor economy and very unscientific.

What is good policy in this respect for the individual is equally good for the home and for business. Many a business concern has gone on the rocks because the proprietor was too much occupied with picayune economies, turning down gas and saving and pinching on petty things, to give his attention to the important things. While saving a trifle here and there, he was losing trade and falling behind in the race, by not putting enough money into his business to keep up with his competitors. While the shortsighted proprietor is hugging pet theories about economy and trying to save on little things, the big things will suffer for a little expenditure which would bring in infinitely greater returns. Liberal expenditure is often the best kind of business economy. Spending precious time and energy in petty savings is often the worst kind of business policy. In order to bring money in one must put out money.

Some people never get out of the world of pennies into the world of dollars. They work so hard to save the cents that they lose the dollars and also the larger growth, the richer experience and the better opportunity.

"The superior man," says Confucius, "is anxious lest he should not get truth; he is not anxious lest poverty should come upon him." Multitudes of people think too much about poverty and economizing. They dwell upon the "can't-afford-it" philosophy, and continually feel the pressure of the rainy-day idea, which has been dinned into their ears from infancy, until it stunts and dwarfs the whole life.

Those who haven't the money cannot, of course, always do that which will contribute to their highest comfort and efficiency; but many people overestimate the advantage of saving a dollar in comparison with their physical well-being. Power is the goal of the highest ambition. Anything which will add to one's power, to one's growth, no matter how much it costs, if it is within possible reach, is worth its price.

We have all met the "can't afford it" men and women who go through life pinching and cheeseparing. We see them stopping at cheap hotels or boarding houses, traveling long distances in the day coach, carrying their lunch with them; seldom or ever buying a newspaper, a magazine, or a book, investing in nothing which will enlarge the mentality or enrich the life; putting every penny they can squeeze out of a very poor living into the bank or in other investments. They may think that what they thus save is going to help their children; but, nevertheless, from every point of view it is very short-sighted economy. I have scarcely ever known an instance where money squeezed out of the real necessities of life was appreciated by the children who inherited it, to say nothing of the dwarfing, impoverishing, aging effect upon those who accumulated it by such self-sacrifice. Oftentimes the hard-earned, sweat-of-the-brow savings have really been a detriment to youthful inheritors, because it has prevented them from using their ability and developing their powers of self-reliance and vigor.

Many families live constantly under the shriveling influence of the stinginess consciousness, the lack and want consciousness, the conviction that the good things of the world were intended for others but not for them. As a result they have never been able to demonstrate anything else but lack, want and limitation. Multitudes of children are reared in this poverty atmosphere, and in time become so convinced that they can't afford things that others have that they never do have them. Their poverty conviction shuts off the supply. They think the little thought and they demonstrate littleness.

Getting along with little and being half-satisfied to continue doing this, generally means that we shall have to get along with less, for it is not a creative mental attitude, not an attitude which attracts plenty and builds success. The "can't afford it" consciousness, the "going without" consciousness, brings you nearer and nearer to the point where you can't afford it, just as the "can afford it" consciousness tends to bring you nearer to the point where you can afford it, for he can who thinks he can, and he can't who thinks he can't. We can't do what we think we can't do; we can't get what we think we can't get.

If you are hard up, you have had a hard-up mind, that is, a hard-up mental attitude, a hard-up conviction, and that has cut off your supply.

The poverty thought, the poverty conviction, is a colossal giant wrestling with human beings and overcoming multitudes of them. It is only those who know the secret hold of the wrestling match, as Dr. W. John Murray says, who can hope to escape the fatal blow of this giant.

I know people in fair circumstances who live so completely in the poverty conviction that they are always hunting for bargains, are always buying cheap things,—cheap food, cheap clothing, cheap furniture, cheap everything. The result is that nothing they have wears or lasts any length of time. While they pinch and screw on prices and think they are saving, they really spend more in the end for poor cheap stuff which is always coming to pieces than they would need to spend on good things, because these would last so much longer than the inferior articles, to say nothing of the infinitely greater satisfaction they would give.

Getting into the current of cheapness not only narrows and pinches the life, but it deteriorates the taste for and appreciation of quality, just as a cheap piano in a home, a piano which is always out of tune, tends to deteriorate the musical taste of the members of the family.

Bargain hunters are nearly always victims of false economy; and women are special offenders in this respect. They will waste hours of precious time, sometimes most of a day, and suffer much discomfort in chasing around from one store to another, looking for bargains and trying to save a few cents on some small purchase they wish to make. Then they will buy wearing apparel and all sorts of articles of inferior material because the price is low, although they know the articles will not wear well. They actually buy, because they are cheap, a great many things they do not need, and then they will probably tell you how much they have saved. If these women would only reckon up what they have expended in this way in one year, they would generally find that, apart altogether from the loss of time and the wear and tear on themselves, they have lost rather than gained on their transactions. They would find that they had spent more than if they had only bought what they really needed, when they needed it, and had paid the regular price for it.

There are many ambitious people with mistaken ideas of economy who very seldom get the kind and quality of food which is capable of building the best blood and the best brain. This going without what would reinforce physical power, create mental force and virility, keeps multitudes of people plodding along in mediocrity who are really capable of doing infinitely better things. This is wretched economy.

The ambitious farmer selects the finest ears of corn and the finest grain, fruits and vegetables for seed. He cannot afford to cumber his precious soil with poor seed. Can the man who is ambitious to make the most of himself afford to eat cheap, stale foods, which lack, or have lost, great energizing elements? Can he

afford to injure his health by trying to save
a little money at the cost of letting the fire
of his energy languish or die?

No one who hopes to accomplish anything in
life can afford to feed his brain with poor fuel.
To do so would be as foolhardy as for a great
factory to burn bad coal on the ground that
good coal was too expensive. Whatever you
do, however poor you may be, don't stint or
try to economize in food fuel, which is the very
foundation and secret of your success in life.
To make a high class man you must have first
class food, and this is not extravagance. You
can't build a superior brain out of cheap, inferior, adulterated foods, gulped down at a
cheap lunch counter.

It is wholly a question of what you get out
of your expenditure, not its amount, that
makes it a wise expenditure or a foolish one.
For instance, it will sometimes pay the biggest kind of returns to pay five or even ten
dollars for a dinner where you can hear great
men with world-wide reputations speak. In
other words, it always pays to get into the most
ambition-arousing and helpful atmosphere
possible. It is a great thing to learn about the

experiences of men who have won out in the very lines in which we are struggling; even if they do not happen to be in our particular line, the principles by which they have succeeded are much the same as those that bring success in any line, and it is extremely valuable to know how they have been applied in any particular instance.

Success attracts success. Money attracts money. Prosperity attracts prosperity, and it pays you to get with people who are prosperous, who have honorably won out in what they attempted. There is a perpetual success suggestion radiating from them which no ambitious young man can afford to lose.

A miserable pinching economy was never intended for God's children. There is a larger and fuller life for them. Man was made for good things, for grand things, to have everything which can minister to his complete growth and development. If he condemns himself to a narrow, unfruitful life of cheeseparing, pinching economies he has no one to blame but himself. Our condition is what our words, our thoughts, our convictions, as well as the result of our efforts, make it. If you are thinking and constantly saying, "I can't afford to do this," or "I can't afford that," "We must make this do," "Money is so scarce," you are sowing the seed which will give you the same kind of a harvest. Your poverty thought will make your future as narrow and limited and poverty-stricken as your present.

CHAPTER XXIII

HOW TO BRING OUT THE MAN YOU CAN BE

We should judge ourselves by what we feel capable of doing, not by what we have done. Nothing else will so nerve you to accomplish greatly as a belief in your own inherent greatness, your godlike possibilities.

There is a potency inside of you which, if you would unlock it, would make of you everything you ever dreamed or imagined you could become.

Don't be afraid to think too highly of yourself. If the Creator made you and is not ashamed of the job, certainly you should not be. He pronounced His work good, and you should respect it.

Persistently hold the thought that you are eternally progressing towards something higher in every atom of your being. This will make you grow, will enrich your life.

The constant struggle to measure up to a high ideal is the only force in heaven or on earth that can make a life great.

That vision which grips your heart, that longing of your soul to do something significant, that dream of high achievement which haunts your imagination, is not a mere fantasy, a whimsical unreality, it is a prophecy of the big things you will do if you get your higher self to work for you.

SAID the great psychologist, William James, "The average individual develops less than ten per cent of his brain cells and less than thirty per cent of his possible physical effi-

315

ciency. We all live below our maximum of accomplishment."

Suppose a human being, because of lack of
proper nourishment, or of some accident in
childhood, should attain only ten per cent of
his possible physical height and only thirty
per cent of his normal weight, what a pitiable
object he would present! What a wretched
apology for the well-proportioned, perfectly
developed being the Creator had planned the
unfortunate dwarf would be!

Yet, so far as the man of the God-plan is
concerned, most of us are self-made dwarfs,
falling short not ten, twenty, or thirty, but a
hundred per cent of our possible development.
Even those who climbed to the mountain
peaks of human achievement,—the Michael
Angelos, the Beethovens, the Shakespeares,
the Miltons, the Dantes, the great men and
women in every field of creative work,—never
reached the maximum of their possible accomplishment.

During a visit to California, I one day stood
in awe before a giant tree, in the hollow of
which General John C. Fremont, "Pathfinder
of the Rockies," with his staff, lived for months

when on a government survey expedition. More than a hundred soldiers had been in the trunk of this tree at one time. Near by was another, over three hundred feet in height, estimated to contain about two hundred thousand feet of lumber,—enough to build all the houses of a small village. As my eye wandered over their huge trunks and limbs, the thought came, that had the same seeds which produced these giants of the forest been planted in a cold northern country, in soil which contained but little nourishment, then, even with the greatest care, they would have been dwarfs instead of giants. Instead of being capable of housing a detachment of soldiers, or of producing enough timber to make houses for a whole village, they would have been mere scrubs of trees, pigmies instead of the giants they might have been under the right conditions for development.

Just as unfavorable conditions in the vegetable kingdom dwarf a possible giant tree and make it a pigmy, so do unfavorable conditions in the animal kingdom dwarf a possible giant in a man and make him a pigmy. But while the tree has no power of itself to change conditions, to alter or improve its environment, man is made to dominate his environment; to bend conditions to his will; to overcome all obstacles that may hinder or delay his highest possible development. In other words, every acorn, if conditions are just right, may become a grand oak, but every human acorn, *in spite of conditions,* no matter how bad they may be, can become, if he will, a grand man.

Man's development depends on his ideal of himself, the mental picture of his appearance and environment which he constantly visualizes. So long as we think that we are merely human, sons of Adam, inheriting only his weaknesses, his limitations; so long as we are convinced that we are helpless victims of heredity, of circumstances and environment, we can never express anything but mediocrity, weakness, inferiority.

A great artist who put his whole soul in his work would never look at inferior pictures, because he said, if he did, he would become familiar with false artistic ideals, and his own pencil would soon catch the taint of inferiority. It is familiarity with a weak, inferior ideal of ourselves that dwarfs and stunts our develop-

ment. As long as we think we are poor inef-
fectual nobodies no power in the world can
make us anything else. Our mental attitude
fixes the limit of our development. Nothing
can save us from our own conviction of inferiority, and inability to rise above the things
that hold us down.

"We actually have powers of many kinds
which we habitually fail to use," says Dr.
James J. Walsh. *"We have acquired the habit
of not being equal to ourselves."* This habit
of not being equal to ourselves is what causes
a great majority of human beings to underes-
timate what they are capable of doing. They
measure their capacity by what they have done
in the past or by what others think they can do,
and so they plod along in a narrow groove of
inferiority, in which their real power is never
exercised. Unless some fortunate accident in-
tervenes, the larger man remains undiscovered,
and they go to their graves without ever having gone below the surface of their almost limitless hidden powers.

I recently met a man who had plodded along
in a very ordinary way through what is com-
monly regarded as the most productive years

of life without showing any special ability.
In fact he failed in several things he had attempted. But, although he was not strong on
self-confidence, he kept hammering away and
happened to make a business hit. His success
aroused a new man in him, gave him a new
sense of power. He was never quite the same
afterwards. He carried himself more confidently, with more assurance. The vision of
new power he had glimpsed in the great within
of himself opened his eyes to his possibilities,
and he rapidly developed a marvelous business
capacity which he never before realized he possessed. His whole outlook and his entire
methods of business changed. Timidity, hesi-
tation, diffidence, a wobbly uncertain policy
of life gave place to boldness, self-confidence,
quickness and firmness of decision, and he went
up by leaps and bounds until he became a great
financial power, and a leader in his community.
He had found the hidden spring which opened
up the gate of his life and gave him a glimpse
of his divine resources.

Not what you have done, or have failed to
do, but what you are capable of doing now;
not what you are, but what you are capable of

becoming,—these are the important facts in your life. It doesn't matter so much what others think of you; what they believe is possible to you; it is what you think of yourself; what you belive you have the ability to do that counts. This is of immense importance to you, because you will not begin to touch your possibilities until you make the acquaintance of your real self, the bigger possible "me" in you.

After his seventy-five years of marvelous individual unfoldment, Thomas A. Edison says that man is yet in the chimpanzee stage of development, and that he has gained but a mere glimpse of his environment.

The unfoldment of man's hidden powers has progressed more rapidly during the past twenty-five years than in any other fifty years of the world's history. But the advance in individual progress is nothing compared with the developments this century will witness. There is no name so secure in the Hall of Fame, there is no leader in any line of endeavor to-day, who is not likely to be superseded by someone who is yet entirely unknown to fame. There may be at this moment, on this continent, some youth who will break all previous records in music, in art or literature. There may be working for some American merchant to-day a clerk who will eclipse the records of the greatest merchant princes of the world. A greater than Shakespeare may now be in swaddling clothes.

When every human being awakens his sleeping genius, brings out the giant in the great within of him, we will have a world of supermen, a race of gods.

John Drinkwater, author of the great play, "Abraham Lincoln," says: "He who most completely realizes himself is he who most fitly assumes leadership of men, not only in the days of his life on earth, but in the story that he becomes thereafter. And for nearly two thousand years there has been no man of whom we have record who has so supremely realized himself to the very recesses of his being as this American, Lincoln."

There is no man, however humble his birth or environment, who brings out the best that is in him, realizes himself "to the very recesses of his being," who will not be a great man. But it is only at long intervals that anyone does this; that a man arises whose full power has been given anything like complete expression as in a Lincoln.

Many of the richest mines in the world were abandoned time and again before their hidden wealth was discovered by the more gritty and persevering prospectors. These men were not satisfied with superficial digging, but went down into the very bowels of the earth until they found the treasure they were after. They became fabulously rich, while the fellows who quit, or wandered from claim to claim, never giving time or energy enough to one; never having enough faith in its possibilities to dig deeper, died in poverty. In one instance I know of a man who mortgaged everything he had in the world, borrowed all he could, and even sold his clothing, to raise enough money to enable him to sink a shaft below the point at which a former prospector had quit, and, going only a few yards deeper, he struck one of the richest silver mines on this continent.

The men who never amount to much, the failures and ne'er-do-wells, are like the prospectors who dug only a little way down into their claims and then quit, dying in poverty

and wretchedness when they might have been
rich beyond their wildest dreams. There are
thousands of down-and-outs in the great failure army to-day who had possibilities that
would have made them captains in the ranks
of industry, leaders in different vocations;
there are multitudes of employees, much abler
men and women than their employers, plodding hopelessly in inferior positions, who have
enough undiscovered ability hidden away in
them to make them supreme in their line, but
they have never had the grit, the courage and
the perseverance to dig down to the treasure
house of their hidden wealth. They prospected
a little along the surface of their being and
then quit.

There is just as much success material; there
are just as many success potencies in many of
those who fail as there are in those who succeed. The trouble with most of the failures
is that they never dig deep enough into themselves to bring out the bigger man that is hidden in them. Multitudes of men and women
never discover their real selves, because their
investigations are so superficial. They don't
think deeply or work in the right way; they

don't focus their efforts with sufficient intensity to open the door to their locked-up possibilities.

Are you willing to go through life as a pigmy when there is something in you which even now is telling you that you can be a giant? Are you going to put forth a giant's efforts to bring out the biggest thing in you, or are you going to sit around waiting for luck or something outside of yourself to come to your assistance,—for outside capital, for somebody to give you a lift?

You will never unfold the bigger man God has wrapped up in you in this way, my friend. The only power that will develop the giant in you is right inside of you. God himself can't develop the human acorn that chooses to remain a dwarf, a scrub oak instead of the grand human oak of the Creator's plan.

THE END

Printed in the United States
52606LVS00001B/103-104

9 780766 178113